MW00710235

Medical Recollections of the Army of the Potomac

MEDICAL RECOLLECTIONS

OF THE

ARMY OF THE POTOMAC.

BY

JONATHAN LETTERMAN, M.D.

LATE SURGEON UNITED STATES ARMY, AND MEDICAL DIRECTOR OF THE ARMY OF
THE POTOMAC.

NEW YORK:
D. APPLETON AND COMPANY,
443 & 445 BROADWAY.
1866.
S

PREFACE.

THE following account of the Medical Department of the Army of the Potomac, has been prepared amidst pressing engagements, in the hope that the labors of the Medical Officers of that Army may be known to an intelligent people, with whom to know is to appreciate; and as an affectionate tribute to many—long my zealous and efficient colleagues—who, in days of trial and danger, which have passed, let us hope never to return, evinced their devotion to their country and to the cause of humanity, without hope of promotion, or expectation of reward.

Near SAN BUENAVENTURA, CAL.,
February 1st, 1866.

MEDICAL RECOLLECTIONS

OF THE

ARMY OF THE POTOMAC.

In obedience to orders from the War Department, dated June 23, 1862, I reported on the 1st day of July to Major-General McClellan at Haxhall's Landing, on the James River, for duty as Medical Director of the Army of the Potomac, and on the 4th took charge of the Medical Department of that army.

On arriving at the White House, June 28th, I found there was no communication between that depot and the headquarters of the army, then *en route* for James River. At the former point I met Mr. Olmstead and several other members of the Sanitary Commission, whose labors, here as elsewhere, were arduous and successful. It was necessary that the medical supplies and the transports for the wounded and sick should be sent up the James River to meet the wants of the army. And as it was impossible to obtain the requisite orders from Dr. Tripler, then Medical Director—as the telegraph wires had been cut—and feeling sure that that experienced officer would approve my exerting authority in such a case, I directed Assistant-Surgeon Alexander, U. S. A., and Assistant-Surgeon Dunster, U. S. A., the Medical Director of Transportation, to proceed up that river with their supplies and vessels with all possible despatch. They reached Harrison's Landing in time to be of the greatest service. The troops for several consecutive days and nights had been march-ing and fighting among the swamps and streams which, abounding in this part of Virginia, render it almost a Serbonian bog. The malaria arising from these hotbeds of disease began to manifest its baneful effects upon the health of the men when they reached Harrison's Landing. The labors of the troops had been excessive, the excitement intense; they were obliged to subsist upon marching rations, and little time was afforded to prepare the meagre allowance. They seldom slept, and even when the opportunity offered, it was to lie in the mud with the expectation of being called to arms at any moment. When it is remembered how short a time this army had been under discipline, we are surprised that it should have

submitted so cheerfully to the orders of the commanding General, and endured the sufferings which, for the
sake of the country, those orders of necessity entailed.
This marching and fighting in such a region, in such
weather, with lack of food, want of rest, great excitement, and the depression necessarily consequent upon
it, could have no other effect than that of greatly increasing the numbers of sick after the army reached
Harrison's Landing. Scurvy existed in the army when
it reached this point. The seeds had doubtless been
planted by want of vegetables, exposure to cold and
wet, working and sleeping in the mud and rain, and
the inexperience of the troops in taking proper care of
themselves under difficult circumstances. This disease
is not to be dreaded merely for the numbers it sends
upon the Reports of Sick : the evil goes much further,
and the causes which give rise to it undermine the
strength, depress the spirits, take away the courage
and elasticity of those who do not report themselves
sick, and who yet are not well. They do not feel sick,
and yet their energy, their powers of endurance, and
their willingness to undergo hardship, are in a great
degree gone, and they know not why. In this way
the fighting strength of the army was affected to a
much greater degree than was indicated by the number of those who reported sick. All these hardships
reacted upon the Medical officers in common with the

rest of the army. A number of them became sick
from the exposure and privations to which they had
been subjected, and those who did not succumb entirely to these influences were worn out by the excessive labor required of them during the Campaign upon
the Peninsula, especially by that incident to the
battles immediately preceding the arrival of the army
at Harrison's Landing. The nature of the military
operations unavoidably placed the Medical Department in a condition far from satisfactory. The supplies had been exhausted almost entirely, or had from
necessity been abandoned—the hospital tents had
been almost universally left behind or destroyed—the
ambulances were not in condition to render effective
service, and circumstances required a much larger
number of Medical officers to perform the duties of
that portion of the Staff. It was impossible to obtain
proper reports of the number of sick in the army
when it reached Harrison's Landing. After about six
thousand had been sent away on the transports, twelve
thousand seven hundred and ninety-five remained.
The data on which to base the precise percentage of
sick and wounded could not then be obtained; but
from the most careful estimate which I could make,
the sickness amounted to at least twenty per cent.
On the 1st of July I directed the " Harrison House "
to be taken and used as an hospital. It was the only

available building in that vicinity, although entirely
inadequate to meet the wants of the army. At that
time only a few wall tents could be obtained with
which to enlarge the capacity of the hospital—no
hospital tents could be procured. The rain began to
fall heavily on the morning of the 2d, and continued
with little interruption until the evening of the 3d.
A few wounded came to the hospital on the 1st, but
on the 2d, and thereafter for several days, they came
in great numbers. Relays of medical officers were
required day and night, and continued to work faithfully until all the wounded who desired assistance had
received it. In the absence of tents no shelter could
be provided, and the vast majority, being slightly
wounded, were obliged to find protection from the
rain as best they could; the more serious cases were
kept in the building. The greatest difficulty experienced at this time was to provide proper food, which
very many needed more than any medical or surgical
aid. Very soon large cauldrons and supplies of beef-
stock were obtained from the Medical Purveyor, and
hard bread from the Commissary Department, by
means of which an excellent soup was prepared and
freely issued, cooks being at first employed night and
day. This hospital was afterwards enlarged by hospital tents so as to contain twelve hundred patients,
and when the army left Harrison's Landing the tents

were removed to Craney Island, near Fortress Monroe,
and an hospital established there by Surgeon Stocker,
U. S. Vols., who conducted the removal and reëstablishment of the hospital speedily and well.   The
transports for the sick and wounded, except those
that had been sent North from the Pamunkey River,
reached the army on the 2d of July.   These vessels
were fitted up with beds, bedding, medicines, hospital
stores, food, with many delicacies, and arrangements
for their preparation; every thing, indeed, that was
necessary for the comfort and well-being of the
wounded and sick.   Surgeons, stewards, and nurses
were assigned to their respective boats, and remained
with them wherever they went.   I doubt if vessels
have ever been so completely fitted up for the transportation of the sick and wounded as these had been
by order of Surgeon-General Hammond.   The shipment of the wounded began on the 2d of July, and was
continued day and night until a very large number had
been sent away.   The want of shelter and proper accommodation at that time rendered it necessary to send
away many who, under more favorable circumstances,
would have been retained with the army.   The weather
was so inclement, the mud so excessive, the shelter so inadequate, that there was an evident disposition on the
part of Medical officers to look leniently upon any
cases of sickness or of wounds.   Had they not been

sent on board, they must have remained without protection from the elements, and without proper food. On the 15th of July about seven thousand had been sent to Fortress Monroe and the North. Much valuable assistance was rendered by a number of medical and other gentlemen who left their homes to alleviate the sufferings of the wounded. Some came apparently for the sake of notoriety, and did nothing; but their shortcomings were atoned for by the good deeds of many others, prominent among whom were Dr. Reed and Dr. McKennan, of Pennsylvania, and Mr. Clement C. Barclay, of Philadelphia, so well known throughout the Army of the Potomac for his active benevolence.

During the first week the shipment of the wounded was in progress, the troops began to feel the effects of miasmatic and other influences, as evinced in the prevalence of malarial fevers of a typhoid type, diarrhœa, and scurvy. My attention was then directed to the most expeditious method of improving the health of the army. The means considered proper for adoption (some of which had already been enforced with great benefit), were set forth in a communication I addressed, on the 18th of July, to Brigadier-General S. Williams, Assistant Adjutant-General. An extract from this communication was, by order of the Commanding General, published to the army in orders, and from this I quote the following:

"The diseases prevailing in our own army are generally of a mild type, and are not increasing; their chief causes are, in my opinion, the want of proper food (and that improperly prepared), exposure to the malaria of swamps, and the inclemencies of the weather, excessive fatigue, and the want of natural rest, combined with great excitement of several days' duration, and the exhaustion consequent thereon. I would recommend, to remedy these evils, that food with abundance of fresh vegetables, shelter, rest with a moderate amount of exercise, be given all the troops, and general and personal police enforced. To accomplish this I would suggest that an abundant supply of fresh onions and potatoes be used by the troops daily for a fortnight, and thereafter at least twice a week, *cost what they may ;* that the dessicated vegetables, dried apples, or peaches, and pickles, be used thrice a week; that a supply of fresh bread, by floating ovens or other methods, be distributed at least three times a week; that the food be prepared by companies and not by squads; and that there be two men detailed from each company as permanent cooks to be governed in making the soups, and cooking by the enclosed directions; that wells be dug as deep as the water will permit; that the troops be provided with tents (or other shelter) to protect them from the sun and rain, which shall be raised daily, and struck once a week and placed upon new ground—the *tentes d'abri* also to be placed over new ground once a week; that men be required to cut pine tops, spread them thickly in their tents, and not sleep on the ground; that camps be formed, not in the woods, but a short distance from them, where a free circulation of pure air can be procured, and where the ground has been exposed to the sun and air to such an extent as to vitiate the noxious exhalations from the human body, and from the decaying vegetation. Sleep during the day will not compensate for the loss of it at night, and I suggest that as far as possible the troops be allowed the natural time for rest; that not more than two drills a day be had, one in the morning from quarter past six to seven o'clock, one in the evening from half past six to quarter past seven o'clock; that the men be allowed to sleep until sunrise, and that they have their breakfast as soon as they rise—this with the labor required for policing will be sufficient during the present season; that when troops march they should have breakfast (if only a cup of coffee) before starting, and after their arrival in camp each man be given a gill of whiskey in a canteen three-fourths filled with water. I would also recommend that the strictest attention be paid to policing, general and special; that all the troops be compelled to bathe once a week, a regiment at a time being marched to the river from a brigade, one hour after sunrise or an hour and a half before sunset, to remain in the water fifteen minutes; that sinks be dug and used, six inches of earth being thrown into them daily, and when filled to within two feet of the surface, new sinks be dug and the old ones to be filled up; that holes be dug at each company kitchen for the refuse matter and filled in like manner; that the entire grounds of each regiment be thoroughly policed every day, and the refuse matter, including that from stables and wagon yards, be buried two feet below the surface, or burned; that dead animals, and the blood and offal from slaughtered animals, be not merely covered with earth, but buried at least four feet under ground; that the spaces between regiments be kept policed, and no nuisance whatever be allowed anywhere within the limits of this army; and that regimental commanders be held *strictly* accountable that this most important matter is attended to. I think if these suggestions be carried into effect, that we may with reason expect the health of this army to be in as good a state as that of any army in the field. Every effort is being made by the Commissary and Quartermaster Departments to provide such articles as I have mentioned belonging to their departments."

This extract will be sufficient to explain the views I entertained on this subject, so vital to the army and the country. On the 2d of July I addressed a letter to Surgeon-General Hammond, asking that one thousand hospital tents, and two hundred ambulances, might speedily be sent for the use of the army. I felt convinced that great destitution in tents would be found to exist, that many ambulances had been lost, and that it would be necessary to replace both these articles. The tents, I considered, would be especially needed to shelter the wounded and sick, whom it would be desirable to keep with the army.

Nothing so disheartens troops, and causes homesickness among those who are well, as sending the sick to the Hospitals outside the army to which they belong; such was the experience of the armies in the Crimea —and it is that of all armies. On the 7th of July the Quartermaster-General at Washington informed me that few hospital tents were on hand, and on the 9th that he had ordered two hundred ambulances from Philadelphia, and two hundred and fifty hospital tents from Washington to Fortress Monroe; and that

the remaining seven hundred and fifty hospital tents
would be forwarded as soon as they were made.
Three hundred of these tents reached Harrison's
Landing on the 18th of July, and on the 1st of
August a large number arrived, which were used for
the sick—the ambulances were distributed before the
army left. Before the communication of July 18th
was written to Brigadier-General Williams, the existence of scurvy attracted my serious attention. I con-
sulted with Colonel Clarke, the chief commissary of
the army, who ordered large supplies of potatoes,
onions, cabbage, tomatoes, squashes, and beets, and
fresh bread. The first arrival of antiscorbutics was
on the 7th of July—potatoes and onions arrived on
the 20th—and thereafter the supplies were so abundant that potatoes, onions, and cabbage rotted at the
wharf, for want of some one to take them away. The
fresh bread was eagerly sought for by the men, who
loathed the hard bread which they had used for so
many weeks. This loathing was no affectation, for this
bread is difficult to masticate—is dry and insipid—
absorbs all the secretions poured into the mouth and
stomach, and leaves none for the digestion of other
portions of the food. In addition to the vegetables
and fresh bread procured by the Commissary Department, fifteen hundred boxes of fresh lemons were
issued by the Medical Purveyor to the various hos-

pitals and to the troops. The beneficial effect of this treatment soon became perceptible in the health of the men, and when we left Harrison's Landing scurvy had disappeared from the Army of the Potomac. In consequence of the authority given me by Surgeon-General Hammond to call directly upon the Medical Purveyors at New York, Philadelphia, and Washington, for all that I considered necessary, the Medical Department of this army was fully supplied with every thing requisite for the proper treatment of the sick and wounded.

Ice was freely supplied to the hospitals and transports. Instructions on the important subject of police were issued, and inspections frequently made by medical officers in the different corps, by officers sent from the Medical Director's office, and by myself, to see that they were enforced. This duty was very laborious during the excessive heat prevailing in July and August. In a few regiments the sickness increased, in others it remained nearly stationary, and in others it decreased one-half; the cases became less severe, yielded more readily to treatment, and on the whole, the health of the army was rapidly improving. It is impossible to convey to any one, not mingling with troops, a correct idea of this improvement. The number reported sick on the regimental returns cannot be taken as the true condition of the health of the army, upon its arrival at that point. The want of proper nourishment, the depressing effects of the climate, and of the labors and anxieties endured, undermined the strength and spirits of a great many who apparently were well, so that the effective strength of the army when it reached Harrison's Landing, and for some time after, was less than the returns would indicate. On the other hand, there are many ways in which improved health manifests itself, which cannot adequately be described. There is so much in the appearance, in the life and vivacity exhibited by men in their slightest actions, even in the voice, which conveys to one's mind the impression of health and spirits, of the presence of vigorous and manly courage, which to be understood must be felt—it cannot be told. The real strength of the army when it left Harrison's Landing was greater than the number reported sick would make it appear. It was agreeable to notice that the measures adopted were so ably and so cordially carried into effect by the Medical Directors of Corps, and their subordinate officers, for to their exertions the improvement in the health of the troops was principally due. From the 15th of July until the 3d of August the transports fitted up for carrying the sick and wounded were employed chiefly in bringing from City Point our wounded who had been taken prisoners during the "Seven

days," andconvey ing them to New York, Philadelphia, Baltimore, and Washington. The first vessels
despatched to City Point conveyed, by direction of
the Commanding General, large supplies of lemons,
brandy, lint, and such articles as were considered
necessary (by the Medical Director) for the comfort
of our men—with a request to the Commander of the
Confederate forces that he would receive them, and
have them distributed: the request was not granted,
and the articles were returned. The reason for this
course may have been satisfactory to the enemy, but
it is difficult to perceive upon what grounds, either of
humanity or military etiquette, it rested. It certainly
could not have taken from his strength to have
allowed these sufferers the comforts which we were
so anxious for them to enjoy. The transports were
stopped at Harrison's Landing, on their way north,
that General McClellan might visit them, and that I
might inspect them, and be certain from personal
observation that every thing was in proper order, and
all supplies and attention given to the wounded that
were necessary for their welfare. Three thousand
eight hundred and forty-five of these prisoners were
comfortably transported in these vessels. The boats,
on their return trips from the north, were loaded
with exchanged Confederate prisoners who were not
sick or wounded, and were employed in this duty

until after the 6th of August.   The condition of these
vessels, on their arrival at Harrison's Landing with
these men, beggars description—filthy beyond conception, and infested with vermin, they stank in
one's nostrils.   In this state they were turned over
again to the Medical Department.   It was just at
this time, and before all the vessels had returned,
that preparations were made for the Army to evacuate
the Peninsula.   A vast amount of labor was required
to place these vessels in even a presentable condition
for the reception of sick and wounded, but the exigencies of the service demanded their immediate use.
The shipment of wounded and sick began on the 3d
of August, at which time but few of the transports
were at my disposal.   The chief Quartermaster, Colonel (now Major-General) Ingalls, gave me every aid
in his power, and placed boats under my orders at
different times.   On the 15th of August, before the
Army left its encampment, over fourteen thousand had
been sent away.   The shipment would have been
much more rapid had the transports remained always under my control.   In one day over five thousand six hundred were sent away.   It is false economy
to use medical transports as vessels for freight, conveying troops, etc., as in this instance—they should
be used for no other purpose than that for which they
are designed.   If they are, the vessels cannot be kept

clean; bedding becomes ruined and lost, even when packed away. The sick and wounded must be sent in more or less haste, which is the cause of another serious evil—the want of time to have the cases that are to be sent away properly examined. From this cause many were taken on board who should not have been received. Many cases were sent from regiments which had marched, by Colonels or Captains (without the knowledge of the Medical officers), who were fully able to perform the duties required of them, and under the circumstances it became necessary to transport them on the boats. There are always numbers of skulkers and worthless men in an army, who are constantly endeavoring to escape duty, and the most common means is to report sick. These are the cases which require most careful examination, and these the men who raise the cry of the inhumanity of Surgeons. Out of three thousand cases examined at Fortress Monroe, Va., upon our arrival there, one-fifth were found fit for duty—an instance of the impolicy of using medical transports for other purposes. I had sent Assistant-Surgeon Thomas McMillin, U. S. A., to Fortress Monroe to superintend the pitching of four hundred and fifty hospital tents near that place, and to make the necessary arrangements for the care of the sick who would be sent there. Assistant-Surgeon McClellan, U. S. A., was directed to take charge of the large and important hospital then in course of construction near the same fortification. Both of these officers acted with energy and judgment, and deserve credit for their efficiency. Every vessel employed in transporting sick and wounded was supplied with Surgeons, cooks, and nurses, and all the necessary appliances. When the time and means are considered, it will, I think, be conceded that seldom has so large a number of sick and wounded been so speedily, so comfortably, and so safely transported. The zeal and ability displayed by Assistant-Surgeon Dunster, U. S. A. (who was in immediate charge of this transportation), cannot be forgotten. The supplies appertaining to the Medical Department, owing to the excellent manner in which the duties of Purveyor were performed by Assistant-Surgeon Alexander, were in every respect ample while we were encamped at Harrison's Landing; and when the army left that place it was, so far as the Medical Department was concerned, fully equipped for another campaign. The subject of the ambulances became, after the health of the troops, a matter of importance. No system had anywhere been devised for their management. They were under the control both of Medical officers and Quartermasters, and, as a natural consequence, little care was exercised over them by either. They could not be depended upon for efficient service in time of action or upon a march, and were too often used as if they had been made for the convenience of commanding officers. The system I devised was based upon the idea that they should not be under the immediate control of Medical officers, whose duties, especially on the day of battle, would prevent any proper supervision; but that other officers, appointed for that especial purpose, should have direct charge of the horses, harness, ambulances, etc., and yet under such regulations as would enable Medical officers at all times to procure them with facility when needed for their legitimate purpose.

Neither the proper kind nor the number of ambulances was in the army at that time, but it was necessary, nevertheless, to devise such a system as would render most available the materials upon the spot without waiting for the arrival of the additional number that had been asked for, only a portion of which ever came.

Under such views I prepared the following system, which, meeting the cordial approval of the Commanding General, was, by his direction, published in orders, viz.:

"HEADQUARTERS, ARMY OF THE POTOMAC,
" *Camp near Harrison's Landing, Va., Aug.* 2, 1862.

"SPECIAL ORDERS,
    No. 147.

"The following regulations for the organization of the ambulance corps and the management of ambulance trains, are published for the information and government of all concerned. Commanders of Army Corps will see that they are carried into effect without delay.

" 1. The ambulance corps will be organized on the basis of a captain to each Army Corps, as the commandant of the ambulance corps; a first lieutenant for a division, second lieutenant for a brigade, and a sergeant for each regiment.

" 2. The allowance of ambulances and transport carts will be: one transport cart, one four-horse and two two-horse ambulances for a regiment; one two-horse ambulance for each battery of artillery; and two two-horse ambulances for the headquarters of each Army Corps. Each ambulance will be provided with two stretchers.

" 3. The privates of the ambulance corps will consist of two men and a driver to each ambulance, and one driver to each transport cart.

" 4. The captain is the commander of all the ambulances and transport carts in the Army Corps, under the direction of the Medical Director. He will pay special attention to the condition of the ambulances, horses, harness, etc., requiring daily inspections to be made by the commanders of the division ambulances, and reports thereof to be made to him by these officers. He will make a personal inspection once a week of all the ambulances, transport carts, horses, harness, etc., whether they have been used for any other purpose than the transportation of the sick and wounded and medical supplies, reports of which will be transmitted, through the Medical Director of the Army Corps, to the Medical Director of the Army every Sunday morning. He will institute a drill in his corps, instructing his men in the most easy and expeditious method of putting men in and taking them out of the ambulances, taking men from the ground, and placing and carrying them on stretchers, observing that the front man steps off with the left foot and the rear man with the right, etc. He will be especially careful that the ambulances and transport carts are at all times in order, provided with attendants, drivers, horses, etc., and the kegs rinsed and filled daily with fresh water, that he may be able to move at any moment. Previous to, and in time of action, he will receive from the Medical Director of the Army Corps his orders for the distribution of the ambulances and the points to which he will carry the

wounded, using the light two-horse ambulances for
bringing men from the field, and the four-horse ones
for carrying those already attended to further to the
rear, if the Medical Director considers it necessary.
He will give his personal attention to the removal of
the sick and wounded from the field and to and from
the hospitals, going from point to point to ascertain
what may be wanted, and to see that his subordinates
(for whose conduct he will be responsible) attend to
their duties in taking care of the wounded, treating
them with gentleness and care, and removing them
as quickly as possible to the places pointed out, and
that the ambulances reach their destination. He will
make a full and detailed report, after every action and
march, of the operations of the ambulance corps.

"5. The first lieutenant assigned to the ambulance corps of a division will have complete control,
under the commander of the whole corps and the
Medical Director, of all the ambulances, transport
carts, ambulance horses, etc., in the division. He will
be the acting assistant quartermaster for the division
ambulance corps, and will receipt and be responsible
for the property belonging to it, and be held responsible for any deficiency in ambulances, transport carts,
horses, harness, etc., pertaining to the ambulance corps
of the division. He will have a travelling cavalry
forge, a blacksmith, and a saddler, who will be under

his orders to enable him to keep his train in order. He will receive a daily inspection report of all the ambulances, horses, etc., under his charge from the officer in charge of brigade ambulance corps; will see that the subordinates attend strictly to their duties at all times, and will inspect the corps under his charge once a week, a report of which inspection he will transmit to the commander of the ambulance corps.

" 6. The second lieutenant in command of the ambulances of a brigade will be under the immediate orders of the commander of the ambulance corps for the division, and have superintendence of the ambulance corps for the brigade.

" 7. The sergeant in charge of the ambulance corps for a regiment will conduct the drills, inspections, etc., under the orders of the commander of the brigade ambulance corps, and will be particular in enforcing rigidly all orders he may receive from his superior officers. The officers and non-commissioned officers of this corps will be mounted.

" 8. The detail for this corps will be made with care by Commanders of Army Corps, and no officer or man will be detailed for this duty except those known to be active and efficient, and no man will be relieved except by orders from these headquarters. Should any officer or man detailed for this duty be found not fitted for it, representation of the fact will be made by the Medical Director of the Army Corps to the Medical Director of this Army.

" 9. Two medical officers from the reserve corps of Surgeons of each division and an hospital steward, who will be with the medicine wagon, will be detailed by the Medical Director of the Army Corps to accompany the ambulance train when on the march, the train of each division being kept together, and will see that the sick and wounded are properly attended to. A medicine wagon will accompany each train.

" 10. The officers connected with the corps must be with the trains on a march, observing that no one rides in the ambulances without the authority of the Medical officers, except in urgent cases; but men must not be allowed to suffer when the Medical officers cannot be found. Use a sound discretion in this matter, and be especially careful that the men and drivers are in their proper places. The place for the ambulances is in front of all wagon trains.

" 11. When in camp the ambulances, transport carts, and ambulance corps will be parked with the brigade, under the supervision of the commander of the corps for the brigade. They will be used on the requisition of the regimental Medical officers, transmitted to the commander of the brigade ambulance corps, for transporting the sick to various points and procuring medical supplies, and for nothing else. The

non-commissioned officer in charge will always accompany the ambulances or transport carts when on this
or any other duty, and he will be held responsible
they are used for none other than their legitimate
purposes. Should any officer infringe upon this order
regarding the uses of ambulances, etc., he will be
reported by the officer in charge to the commander of
the train, all the particulars being given.

"12. The officer in charge of a train will at once
remove every thing not legitimate, and if there be not
room for it in the baggage wagons of the regiment,
will leave it on the road. Any attempt by a superior
officer to prevent him from doing his duty in this or
any other instance, he will promptly report to the
Medical Director of the Army Corps, who will lay the
matter before the Commander of the Corps. The latter
will, at the earliest possible moment, place the officer
offending in arrest for trial for disobedience of orders.

"13. Good serviceable horses will be used for the
ambulances and transport carts, and will not be taken
for any other purpose, except by orders from these
headquarters.

"14. The uniform of this corps is—for privates, a
green band, two inches broad, around the cap, a green
half-chevron, two inches broad, on each arm above the
elbow, and to be armed with revolvers; non-commissioned officers to wear the same band around the cap

as the privates, chevrons two inches broad, and green, with the point toward the shoulder, on each arm above the elbow.

"15. No person will be allowed to carry from the field any wounded or sick except this corps.

"16. The commanders of the ambulance corps, on being detailed, will report without delay to the Medical Director at these headquarters for instructions. All division, brigade, or regimental Quartermasters having any ambulances, transport carts, ambulance horses, or harness, etc., in their possession, will turn them in at once to the commander of the division ambulance corps.

"By command of Maj.-Gen. McCLELLAN.

"(Signed)   S. WILLIAMS,
        Assistant Adjutant-General."

This system being entirely new, much labor was necessary to put it in operation; and as the order was not received from the printer's until a few days before we left Harrison's Handing, there were many details that could not be enforced. Imperfectly as the order was carried into effect on our march from the James River to Yorktown and Fortress Monroe, I felt convinced from what I saw of the operation of the system that, when fully understood and carried out, the ambulances would be of much greater service to the wounded and sick. I have been informed that the contrast exhibited (during the battles fought by Major-General Pope in the latter part of August, 1862) between the action of the ambulances belonging to the Army of the Potomac and those corps in which this system did not exist, was very striking in favor of the former. At the battle of Fredericksburg, on the 13th of December, 1862, this system was, for the first time, put into operation and severely tested, and, as will be seen hereafter, it satisfactorily met the demands made upon it. Every thing having been done, while at Harrison's Landing, that was considered necessary and that time permitted, to place the Medical Department in a condition for active service, little was required of me during the march to Fortress Monroe, which began on the 16th of August, nor did any thing worthy of mention occur. While the Army was at Harrison's Landing I inspected the hospitals at Point Lookout, Fortress Monroe, and its immediate vicinity, Portsmouth and Newport News, which were within the jurisdiction of the Army of the Potomac. These hospitals, in August, contained somewhat over seven thousand patients, who required for their care sixty-six surgeons, over five hundred nurses, besides medical cadets, stewards, and cooks. Orders were given for the transportation of the Army by water to another part of Virginia, and all the

vessels that could be obtained, medical transports as
well as others, were pressed into service by the Quartermaster's Department. Rapidity of movement being
required, the troops were sent off with scarcely any
of their ordinary baggage, the ambulances with their
equipments were left behind to be sent after the
troops as vessels could be spared for that purpose.
A large portion of the medical supplies were also left
behind, and, in some cases, every thing but the hospital knapsacks, by orders of colonels of regiments,
quartermasters, and others; in some instances without
the knowledge of the medical officers, in others notwithstanding their protest. It would appear that many
officers consider medical supplies to be the least important in an army; the transportation of their baggage
is of much more pressing necessity than the supplies
for the wounded; and medical officers have been frequently censured (as they were shortly afterwards) for
want of articles required in time of action, when these
have been left behind, or thrown upon the roadside,
by orders they were powerless to resist. From the
date of the embarkation of the troops at Fortress
Monroe to the period when General McClellan was
placed in command of the defences of Washington, I
know little, personally, of the Medical Department of
the Army of the Potomac, as it was not under my
control. On the 2d of September it came again

under my direction, and I found it in a deplorable condition. The officers were worn out by the excessive and harassing labors they had undergone during the time they were attached to the Army of Virginia. A large portion of their supplies had been left behind, as I have said, at Fortress Monroe, and even much of what they had brought was thrown away by commanding officers when on the way to join General Pope. The labor expended at Harrison's Landing in rendering this Department efficient for active service, seemed to have been expended in vain, and it required to be completely refitted before it would be again in proper condition. The circumstances in which the Army of the Potomac and the Army of Virginia (both of which now came under the command of General McClellan) were placed, made this impossible. As soon as the troops reached the defences of Washington, they were marched into Maryland, and no time was allowed Medical officers again to equip themselves with the medicines, instruments, and stores requisite for another campaign. In a few instances the Medical officers who returned with the first troops procured some supplies. Some troops which did not belong to the Army of the Potomac when it lay at Harrison's Landing were also marched rapidly into Maryland. I could know nothing of the condition of *their* Medical Department, except what I

3

learned on the way to meet the enemy, who had
crossed to the north bank of the Potomac. The Med·
ical Department of the entire Army had to be reor·
ganized and resupplied while upon a rapid march in
different sections of the country, and almost in the
face of the enemy. I had ordered a number of
"hospital wagons" from Alexandria, Virginia, which
reached me after we left Washington, and were at
once distributed to different corps. While at Rock·
ville, Maryland, I directed the Medical Purveyor at
Baltimore to put up certain supplies and have them
ready to send to such place as I should indicate. It
was impossible at that time to know the proper place
to direct them to be sent. Two hundred ambulances
were received just before we reached Frederick, Mary·
land, and distributed among the corps. On the 13th
of September we arrived at this city (having left
Washington on the evening of the 7th), where we
found the Ninth Corps, under the command of General Burnside. The enemy held possession of this
place the day before the Commanding General arrived,
and had taken or destroyed the greater portion of the
medical supplies found there. I directed the establishment of hospitals in that city for the wounded in
the battles which were imminent—ordered the supplies to be sent from Baltimore, and sent for a large
amount of articles, in addition, for the field and hos-

pitals. The railroad from Baltimore was not in good condition, and many complaints were made to me of the failure of the company in forwarding the supplies. The railroad bridge over the Monocacy Creek, between Baltimore and Frederick, had been destroyed by the enemy, and all the supplies of the different departments were removed from the cars at this point, four miles from Frederick. A great deal of confusion and delay was the consequence, which greatly embarrassed the Medical Department; and this embarrassment was increased by the fact that cars loaded with supplies were, on some occasions, "switched off" and left for some time (when their arrival was all-important) on the side of the road, to make way for other stores. Some of the articles ordered, I have been informed, never left the railroad depot in Baltimore; they certainly never reached Frederick.

The battle of South Mountain took place on the 14th of September. The village of Middletown, about four miles in the rear of the scene of action, was examined before the battle began, to ascertain its capacities for the care of the wounded. Churches and other buildings were taken as far as was necessary, and as little inconvenience as possible given to the citizens. The Medical Directors of the Corps engaged were instructed to take the houses and barns (the latter being in that region large and commodious, and

well suited to the purpose), in the most sheltered
spots in the rear of their respective commands, for
field hospitals. This was done, and there the wounded received their first and necessary dressings, after
which they were removed to Middletown. The
battle lasted until after dark. From the point, in an
open field, selected by General McClellan as his headquarters, a complete view of the movements of the
troops and the progress of the battle was obtained.
Our wearied men pressed forward courageously, and
climbed the mountain without faltering, knowing well
they would meet at the summit the enemy flushed
with victory. And when the sun went down, the
continual flashing of musketry from General Gibbon's
brigade (as it pushed up the valley leading to the
pass from which we wished to dislodge the enemy),
making darkness visible, added greatly to the beauty
of the scene. As soon as the firing ceased I returned
to Middletown, visited all the hospitals, and gave
such directions as were required for the better care of
the wounded. As I was obliged to leave on the following day, I directed Assistant-Surgeon Thomson,
U. S. A., to take charge of all the hospitals. Surgeons Heard, Pineo, and Nordquist were sent there to
consult with him, and to perform such operations as
the cases demanded. The object in sending these
officers was to have all the required operations done

as speedily as possible, as it would be beyond the power of the surgeons in charge of the different hospitals to perform all in season, and to attend to the other duties required of them. The labors of these officers, here as elsewhere, were skilfully performed. As I anticipated, the wounded, under the supervision of Dr. Thomson, who labored with so much diligence and so much effect, were attended with great care and skill, and the hospitals soon placed in excellent order. This officer may feel well repaid for all the difficulties he encountered, by the complimentary manner in which the President, when on his way to the battle-field of Antietam, spoke of the condition of these hospitals, and the great care taken of the wounded in them. Much kindness was shown to our wounded by the citizens of the village, especially the ladies, until the hospitals were broken up. The battle of Crampton's Gap was fought also on the 14th of September, and was in reality a part of the battle of South Mountain. The hospitals were located in Burkettsville, a village about a mile in the rear of our line; as in Middletown churches and other buildings were selected and fitted up for the wounded by Surgeon White, United States Army Medical Director of the Sixth Corps, who had charge of the Medical Department in this action. A very short time was given to prepare hospitals in either of these villages, as the troops marched from

Frederick and fought these battles on the same day. By the exertions of the Medical officers, some of whom were among the prominent surgeons in the army, the hospitals at Burkettsville were soon in good order, and every care was taken of the wounded. The surgeon in charge, having been guilty of improper conduct, was relieved by Assistant-Surgeon Dubois, U. S. A., who administered these hospitals, as I found from personal inspections, with credit to himself, and to my entire satisfaction. The want of reliable medical reports of these battles prevents my giving the true number of wounded, but the best information I could obtain placed it at twelve hundred and fourteen in both engagements. The Medical Department had not, at this time, been reorganized, and correct reports could not be procured. The army pushed on rapidly, passing, on the 15th, through the village of Boonsboro', which was examined to ascertain the accommodations it afforded for hospital purposes, should I find it necessary to use them. In the afternoon of the same day we marched through Keedysville, which was subjected to a similar examination. Passing beyond this village we came, about sunset, upon the ground afterwards so widely known as the battle-field of Antietam; and were unpleasantly greeted by the shells from one of the enemy's batteries, which opened upon us as soon as we appeared in sight. The resources of the country for hospital purposes were ascertained as speedily as possible, and, when an idea was given of the nature of the battle, and the positions to be occupied by our troops, instructions were issued to Medical Directors of Corps to form their hospitals, as nearly as possible, by divisions, and at such a distance in the rear of the line of battle as to be secure from the shot and shell of the enemy—to select the houses and barns most easy of access—and, when circumstances permitted, to choose barns well provided with hay and straw, as preferable to houses, since they were better ventilated, and enabled Medical officers to attend a greater number of wounded—to place the wounded in the open air near the barns, rather than in badly-constructed houses—and to have the medical supplies taken to the points indicated. These directions were generally carried into effect, but the hospitals were not always beyond the reach of the enemy's guns. Very few hospital tents were on hand, owing to the haste with which the army moved from Virginia into Maryland, but fortunately the weather after the battle was so pleasant, that the wounded could be well cared for without them. Some fighting took place on the evening of the 16th, and, early in the morning of the 17th of September, the battle of Antietam began, and continued until dark. No one

engaged on that hotly-contested field can ever forget
the intense interest with which he watched the progress of that battle, upon the issue of which the welfare of his country so much depended; this feeling
was magnified by the knowledge that our troops
were fighting an enemy by whom they had been defeated a few days before. I received valuable aid on
this occasion from Assistant-Surgeon Howard, U. S.
A., who was busily engaged, while the battle was in
progress, in riding to different parts of the field, and
keeping me informed of the condition of the Medical
Department. After night I inspected all the hospitals in Keedysville, and gave such surgical aid and
instructions as were required. Medical and surgical
supplies were, in this battle, from the causes I have
already given, matters of serious consideration. The
condition of affairs at Monocacy Creek had not improved, and the railroad was not equal to the demands made upon it. The "hospital wagons"
obtained from Alexandria gave a supply of the requisite articles, and enabled surgeons to attend the
wounded as soon as the battle opened. After the
victory was won, medicines, stimulants, dressings,
etc., etc., were brought from Frederick in ambulances
(as no wagons could be procured), and distributed to
the hospitals. The difficulty of obtaining these supplies from the depot was well known, and it caused

much uneasiness to many Medical officers, who were not aware of the successful efforts made, before, during, and after the battle, to supply their wants. The line of battle was between six and seven miles in length, the hospitals were therefore very numerous; but, though I was constantly occupied in visiting them, I did not find the stores exhausted—the supply of some articles was, in particular instances, very much diminished; but a sufficient quantity of such articles as were necessary, from time to time, arrived at the temporary depot established at Sharpsburg shortly after the battle; and when it was broken up, about the middle of October, a portion of the supplies remained. Not only were *our* wounded supplied, but the wounded of the enemy, who fell into our hands, were furnished with all the medical and surgical appliances required for their use. In all battles it is an object of the first consideration to supply the troops with ammunition and food—to these every thing must give way, and become of secondary importance. For this reason the difficulty of supplying the hospitals with food was much greater than that of providing articles belonging to the Medical Department—and, although foreign to the duty of this department, seriously affected it. The real depots of supplies, for all departments of this Army, were in Washington and Baltimore, and in conse-

quence of the distance, and the causes to which I
have alluded, great difficulty was found in supplying
the troops. I procured an order from Colonel (now
Major-General) Ingalls, for twelve wagons to be
turned over by the Quartermaster at Frederick to an
officer I should send there for medicines and food;
but the wagons could not be found there, and only
two could be obtained at headquarters, which were
sent under a Medical officer, and loaded with coffee,
sugar, and bread. This difficulty lasted only a short
time, after which, owing to the exertions of the Chief
Commissary, Colonel Clarke, the hospitals were abundantly supplied. I have mentioned that the ambulances had been left at Fortress Monroe when the
troops embarked, and that no system existed, except
in the corps which formed the Army of the Potomac
at Harrison's Landing. Only a portion of those
belonging to some of the corps arrived in time for
the battle—some were lost in a storm on the Chesa-
peake Bay; and although two hundred had been distributed just before the action, they were unorganized.
I did not, under these circumstances, expect them to
prove very efficient. Notwithstanding the condition
of this important branch of the Medical Department,
the wounded were brought from our right before
two o'clock the day following the battle. The Second
Corps was, from the exertions of Captain Garland,

who had charge of the ambulances, more fully equipped than any other corps, and its wounded were removed from the field with care and despatch. The troops on our left were those among whom no system existed, but the Medical officers endeavored to atone by their exertions for this want, and were more successful than I anticipated. No fighting took place on the 18th, both armies preserving the lines they held on the previous evening; while the battle was in progress, the lines were changed as one or the other gave way—so that, in the space between the lines, there was quite a number of wounded who could not be removed until the enemy was forced from his position. In this, as in all battles, there were cases of individual suffering which, perhaps, might have been prevented; and doubtless some men, having been overlooked, remained on the field after the others had been removed. But these instances were rare, when we consider the imperfect manner in which the details of the ambulance system were carried out. For the reasons I have given, it is impossible there should not be cases of suffering, the remedies for which suggest themselves when looking back upon the scene of action. It is well to remember that no system devised by man can be *perfect*, and that no such system, even if it existed, could be carried out perfectly by human agency. Calling to mind the

fact that the ambulance system, imperfect as it may
be found, could not be fully put into practice—
remembering the magnitude of the engagement, the
length of time the battle lasted, and the obstinacy
with which it was contested—it affords me much grati-
fication to state that so few instances of apparently
unnecessary suffering were found to exist after that
action, and that the wounded were removed from that
sanguinary field in so careful and expeditious a manner.   The returns of wounded were very meagre and
imperfect, from the same causes as at South Mountain and Crampton's Gap: they gave in this battle
a total of eight thousand three hundred and fifty,
but there were many cases of slight wounds not
recorded.   The removal of such a large number of
wounded from the field to the General Hospitals was
an arduous undertaking.   The railroad from Green-
castle, Penn., could not be depended upon.   That
from Harper's Ferry was in no better condition; it
was therefore necessary that the wounded should be
sent in ambulances to Frederick, for transportation
to Baltimore, Washington, and elsewhere.   It was
imperative that the trains should leave at the proper
hours, no one interfering with another; that they
should halt at Middletown, where food and rest, with
such surgical aid as might be required, could be given
to the wounded; that food should always be prepared

at this village at the proper time, for the proper number; that the hospitals in Frederick should not be overcrowded, and the ambulances should arrive at the railroad depot in Frederick at the required time to meet the Baltimore trains. With rare exceptions this was accomplished, and all the wounded, whose lives would not be jeopardized, were sent carefully away. Surgeon J. J. Milhau, U. S. A., was placed in charge of the Frederick Hospitals, to which were added two large camps of hospital tents, each capable of accommodating one thousand patients. On the 30th of October the hospitals of this city contained over five thousand patients, attended by sixty-two surgeons, fifteen medical cadets, twenty-two hospital stewards, five hundred and thirty-nine nurses, and one hundred and twenty-seven cooks. No one, who saw them after they were established, can form any conception of the labor required to put them in operation. Every thing had to be, as it were, created; the place itself supplied nothing but some buildings. These hospitals, as I found from personal inspection, were in excellent order, and the wounded attentively and skilfully treated. The zeal and ability displayed by Surgeon Milhau reflect great credit upon him, and the hearty coöperation he invariably gave me, calls up the most pleasing recollections. Measures had been at once taken to gather in from the field,

over which they lay scattered in all directions, such
of the wounded as the enemy had left behind, in his
nocturnal retreat from Antietam, and to place them
where they could be properly attended. Surgeon
Rauch, U. S. Volunteers, was assigned to the duty of
superintending these prisoners, who numbered over
two thousand (notwithstanding the assertion of
Heros (!) Von Borcke that General Lee left only three
hundred on the field). I detailed a sufficient number
of our own medical officers, and directed all the medical officers of the enemy, who had been left behind,
to report to Surgeon Rauch, to whom ambulances
and all necessary supplies were given; of these he
availed himself with his well-known ability; the
wounded were soon placed in the most eligible locations, and every thing done to alleviate their sufferings. Humanity teaches that a wounded and pros-
trate foe is no longer an enemy. There were many
men seriously wounded in this action, whose lives
would have been endangered by removal to General
Hospitals. To give such sufferers every opportunity
of recovery, I established, shortly after this battle,
two large camp hospitals, capable of containing about
one thousand patients. These institutions were the
first of the kind attempted in this country, and were
successful: the larger, named the Antietam Hospital,
established at Smoketown for the wounded on our

right wing, contained about six hundred beds: the other was pitched in an eligible position, in the rear of the left wing: to these all the most serious cases were carried by hand. The inspections I made of these hospitals on various occasions, before the Army recrossed the Potomac, gave me much pleasure, and demonstrated the propriety of their establishment. Surgeon Vanderkieft, U. S. Volunteers, in charge of the Antietam Hospital, manifested a degree of professional skill and executive ability which fully justified my selection of that officer. Immediately after the battle, many persons came within our lines to remove their relatives or friends who had been injured—whose lives, in many instances, depended upon their remaining at rest. It was impossible to convince them that the removal of a dangerously wounded man would be made at the risk of his life —that risk they were perfectly willing to take, if he could only (at the end perhaps of a long and painful journey) be placed in a house. No greater mistake could be made; for the results of that battle gave additional evidence of the absolute necessity of a full, and constantly renewed supply of fresh air to a wounded man—a supply which cannot be obtained in the most perfectly constructed building. A marked contrast could be seen, within a few yards, between the wounded in houses and barns, and those in the open air. Those in houses progressed less favorably than those in barns, those in the latter buildings less favorably than those in the open air; though all were treated alike in other respects. From the frequent inspections I made of the field hospitals, and from the manner in which Medical officers performed their duties, it gives me great pleasure to state that the wounded had every care bestowed upon them—that they were willingly, promptly, and efficiently attended—and I cannot refrain from mentioning here the untiring devotion shown to the wounded of that day. Until all were finally removed, no pains were spared, no labors avoided by the Medical Staff of this Army, to alleviate the sufferings of the thousands who looked to them for relief. A few delinquencies occurred, but they might well be forgotten among the intelligent exertions of the many. Much misrepresentation of the conduct and skill of Medical officers on this field was scattered broadcast over the land, causing heart-rending anxiety to those who had friends or relatives in the Army, who might at any moment require the services of a surgeon. It is certainly true that some incompetent surgeons were commissioned in this Army (chiefly through political and family influence); but sweeping denunciations against an entire class, -composed principally of the rising

medical talent of the country, do great injustice to a
body of men who will compare favorably, in diligence and skill, with the military surgeons of any
nation. Some Medical officers lost their lives in their
devotion to duty on the battle-field of Antietam,
others became ill from the excessive labor which they
conscientiously and skilfully performed. The un-
timely deaths of Surgeon White, of the Regular Army,
Assistant-Surgeon Revere, of the Twentieth Massachusetts Volunteers, and Assistant-Surgeon Kendall,
of the Twelfth Massachusetts Volunteers, by the
hands of the enemy, should not be forgotten by a grate-
ful people; their high sense of duty, professional ability, and unfailing courtesy will certainly be long remembered by their comrades on that field. I had
more ample opportunities than any one else to form a
correct opinion of the surgery of that battle; and if
any fault could be found, it was that "conservative surgery" was practised too much, and the knife not
used enough. Several eminent medical gentlemen
from New York and other cities arrived soon after
the battle, and gave their services to the wounded.
Surgeon-General Hammond, accompanied by Brigadier-General Muir, Deputy Medical Inspector-General of the British Army, visited the field, inspected the hospitals, and gave the sufferers the
benefit of their professional skill. The latter accom-

4

plished officer expressed the pleasure it afforded him to see the manner in which the wounded were attended, and remarked that although he had been on many battle-fields, he had never found them more carefully provided for, or attentively treated.

Dr. Agnew, of New York, came as the representative of the Sanitary Commission, and freely distributed the stores of that organization. Dr. Steiner, of Frederick, was the agent in that city, and was busily engaged in the same deeds of kindness. The private and official acts of these gentlemen were so invariably courteous as to win the esteem of the Medical officers with whom they heartily coöperated. Early in September the General Hospitals in and around Washington came under my control, and were, at my request, placed in charge of Surgeon R. O. Abbott, U. S. A., Assistant Medical Director. The following table will exhibit the number of hospitals, and other matters of interest connected with them:

Number of hospitals.	Number of Med'l officers.	Remaining in hospitals Aug. 31, 1862.	Number of patients admitted.	Total.	Returned to duty.	Discharged.	Deserted.	Sent to other hospitals.	Sent on furlough.	Died.	Remaining Dec. 31, 1862.
85	224	11,797	43,773	55,570	12,200	5,454	973	19,708	2,099	2,634	12,452

The system introduced in the management of these hospitals cannot be too highly commended or too often followed, and must increase the high reputation deservedly enjoyed by that officer.

After these battles the Army remained for some time in Maryland, preparing for another campaign in Virginia. During this time I was chiefly engaged in reorganizing the Medical Department. Hitherto medical supplies for three months had been furnished directly to regiments, and no wagons allowed expressly for their transportation. From these causes large quantities were lost, and in various ways wasted; and not unfrequently all the supplies of a regiment were thrown away by commanding officers, almost in sight of the enemy, that the wagons might be used for other purposes. I desired to reduce the waste which took place when a three months' supply was issued to regiments, to have a small quantity given them at one time, and to have it at all times replenished without difficulty; to avoid a multiplicity of accounts, and yet preserve a proper degree of responsibility; to have a fixed amount of transportation set apart for carrying these supplies, and used for no other purpose. To accomplish these objects the entire system then in vogue must be abolished. On the 4th of October, 1862, I instituted the system of "brigade supplies;" and the following circular, issued at this time, will show the manner in which the Army was supplied thereafter:

"MEDICAL SUPPLY TABLE FOR THE ARMY OF THE POTOMAC FOR
FIELD SERVICE.

"Experience has shown that the medical supply
authorized by the Regulations for a regiment for three
months is too cumbrous for active operation, instances
being frequent where the whole supply has been left
on the roadside. Hereafter, in the Army of the
Potomac, the following supplies will be allowed to a
brigade for one month for active field service, viz.:

"One hospital wagon, filled.

"One medicine chest for a regiment, filled.

"One hospital knapsack for each regimental Medical officer, filled.

"The supplies in the list marked 'A' to be transported in a four-horse wagon.

"The Surgeon in charge of each brigade will require and receipt for all these supplies, including
those in the hospital wagon, and will issue to the
senior Surgeon of each regiment the medicine chest
and knapsacks, taking receipts therefor. The hospital
wagon, with its horses, harness, etc., will be receipted
for by the ambulance quartermaster.

"The Surgeon in charge of the brigade will issue
to the Medical officers of the regiments such of these
supplies as may be required for their commands, in-

formally, taking no receipts, demanding no requisition, but accounting for the issues as expended.

"The Surgeons in charge of brigades will at once make out requisitions in accordance with these instructions, and transmit them, approved by the Medical Directors of Corps, to the Medical Purveyor of this Army. These supplies being deemed sufficient for one month only, or for an emergency, Medical Directors of Corps will see that they are always on hand, timely requisitions being made for that purpose.

ARTICLES.	In Hospital Wagon.	A In four-horse Wagon.	ARTICLES.	In Hospital Wagon.	A In four-horse Wagon.
MEDICINES.			Ex. belladonnæ,	1 oz.	
			" col. rad. fl.,	4 "	
Acaciæ pulvis,	½ lb.		" colocynth. comp.,	8 "	
Acid. sulph. aromat.	½ "		" cinchonæ fl.,	1 lb.	
" tannic,	1 oz.		" ipecac. fl.,	½ "	
Aether sulphuric,	2 lbs.		" zingiberis fl.,	½ "	
" spirit. comp.,	1 "	1 lb.	Ferri chlorid. tinc.,	½ "	1 lb.
" " nitrici,	2 "	2 "	" et quiniæ cit.,	1 oz.	
Alcohol,	12 pts.		" persulphat. liq.,	4 "	
Alumen,	½ lb.		" " pulv.,	1 "	1 "
Ammoniæ carb.,	½ "		Glycerina,	½ lb.	
" liquor,	2 "	4 "	Hydrarg. chlor. mit.,	½ "	
Ant. et Pot. tart.,	1 oz.		" pillulæ,	½ "	
Argent. nitras,	1 "		" unguent.,	1 "	
" " fusus,	1 "		" " nit.,	¼ "	
Brominii, Bibron's antid.,	1 bot.		Iodinum,		8 oz.
Camphora,	½ lb.		Ipecac. et opii pulv.,	¼ "	2 lbs.
Cantharidis,	½ "		" pulvis,		1 "
Cera alba,	¼ "		Lini pulvis,	8 lbs.	
Ceratum simplex,	3 "	12 "	Magnesiæ sulphas,	8 "	20 "
" resinæ,	1 "		Morphiæ,	¼ oz.	4 oz.
Cinchonæ sulphas,	24 oz.		Oleum olivæ,	2 qts.	4 qts.
Chloroformum,	2 lbs.		" ricini,	4 "	4 "
Collodium,	1 oz.		" menth. pip.,		2 oz.
Copaiba,	2 lbs.		" terebinthinæ,	1 "	
Creasotum,	4 oz.		" tiglii,	1 oz.	
Cupri sulphas,	2 "		Opii pulvis,	½ lb.	2 lbs.
Ex. aconit. rad. fl.,	4 "		" pillulæ,	8 doz.	24 doz.

ARTICLES.	In Hospital Wagon.	In four-horse Wagon.
Opii tinctura,	1 lb.	
" " camphora,	1 "	
Pil. cathart. comp.,	8 doz.	24 doz.
" camph. (2 grs.) and opium (1 gr.),	8 "	
" ipecac. (¼ gr.) ex. col. c. (3 grs.),	8 "	
Plumbi acetas,	½ lb.	2 lbs.
Potass. bicarb.,	½ "	2 "
" chlorat.,	½ "	2 "
Potassii sod.,	½ "	2 "
Quiniæ sulphas,	12 oz.	48 oz.
" " in pills (3grs),	8 doz.	24 doz.
Rhei pulvis,		1 lb.
Sapo,	8 lbs.	4 "
Scillæ syrupus,	4 "	
Sinapis nig. pulv.,	6 "	6 lbs.
Sodæ chlor. liq.,	1 bot.	4 bot.
" bicarbon.,	½ lb.	4 lbs.
" et potass. tart.,	1 "	
Spirit. frum. (whiskey),	24 bot.	24 bot.
" vini gallici,	6 "	24 "
Zinci chlor. liq.,	1 lb.	
" sulphas,	1 oz.	1 lb.

HOSPITAL STORES.

ARTICLES.	In Hospital Wagon.	In four-horse Wagon.
Arrow root,	10 lbs.	
Beefsteak, 2 lb. cans,		4 doz.
Candles, sperm,	2 "	12 lbs.
Farina,	10 "	
Nutmegs,	4 oz.	
Sugar, white,	12 lbs.	
Tea, black,	4 "	

INSTRUMENTS.

ARTICLES.	In Hospital Wagon.	In four-horse Wagon.
Buck's Spongeholder,	No. 1	
Cupping Tins,	" 12	
Lancets, thumb,	" 2	
Pocket cases,	" 1	
Probangs,	" 12	
Scarificators,	" 2	
Scissors,	" 2	
Stethoscopes,	" 1	
Syringes, self-injecting,	" 1	
" enema (16 oz.),		No. 4
" hard rubber(4oz.),	" 1	
" penis glass,	" 6	

ARTICLES.	In Hospital Wagon.	In four-horse Wagon.
Syringes, penis, rubber,		No.8
Teeth extracting, sets	No. 1	
Tongue depressor, h'g'd,	" 1	
Tourniquets, field,	" 8	" 8
" screw,	" 2	" 4
Trusses,	" 4	" 16

DRESSINGS, ETC.

ARTICLES.	In Hospital Wagon.	In four-horse Wagon.
Adhesive plaster,	5 yds.	20 yds.
Binders' boards, 2¼ by 12 in.,	8	48
Cotton bats,	2	4
" wadding,	1 sheet	
Flannel red,	4 yds.	
Gutta percha cloth,	2 "	
Ichthyocolla plaster,	10 "	20 yds.
Needles 25, cotton 1 sp'l, thimble 1, in one case,	1	
Oiled muslin,	7 yds.	
" silk,	2¼ "	20 "
Pencils, hair,	No. 12	
Plaster of Paris, grou'd,		50 lbs.
Pins, papers,	2 pap's	4 pap's
Roller bandages, ass'd,	16 doz.	100 dz.
Silk, green (for shades),	1 yd.	
" surgeons'	¼ doz.	4 oz.
Splints,	1 set.	4 sets
" Smith's anterior,		No. 20
Sponge, fine,	½ lb.	1 lb.
Suspensory bandages,	No. 8	No. 16
Tape,	4 piec's	
Thread, linen,		1 lb.
Tow,	10 lbs.	
Towels,	No. 12	No. 40
Twine,	½ lb.	

BOOKS, ETC.

ARTICLES.	In Hospital Wagon.	In four-horse Wagon.
U. S. Dispensatory,	1 copy	
Surgery, Erichsen's,	1 "	
" Smith's H'db'k,	1 "	
" Sargent's Minor	1 "	
Gun-shot wounds, Long-more,	2 "	
Blank books,	1 "	8 cop's
" quarto,	1 "	
Case book,	1 "	
Register of patients,	1 "	

ARTICLES.	In Hospital Wagons.	In Four-horse Wagons.	ARTICLES.	In Hospital Wagons.	In Four-horse Wagons.
Order and Letter Book,			Bed pans, metal,		No. 12
Reg. Returns & Reports,	1 copy		Buckets, leather,	No. 2	8 doz.
Ink (2 oz. bottles),	No. 2	No. 8	Corks, assorted,	8 doz.	No. 4
Inkstand, travelling,	" 1		Corkscrews,	No. 1	
Envelopes,	" 100	" 100	Funnels, ¼ pt., glass,	" 1	
Paper, wrapping, white			Grater, nutmeg,	" 1	
and blue,	2 quir's	2 quir's	Hatchet,	" 1	
" writing,	4 "	8 "	Hone,	" 1	" 12
Pens, steel, with hold's,	1 doz.	4 doz.	Kettles, camp, (2 gals.)		" 12
Pencils, lead,	No. 6		Lanterns, glass,	" 3	
Portfolio,	" 1		Measures, grad. (2 oz.)	" 1	
Sealing wax,	1 stick		" " min.	" 1	
Mucilage,	1 bot.		Medicine measur'g glass,	" 1	
			Mill, coffee,	" 1	
			Mortar and pestle,	" 1	
BEDDING, ETC.			Pill boxes,	2 pap's	
			" tiles,	No. 1	
Blankets,	No. 20	No. 40	Razor and strop, in case,	" 1	
Gutta percha bed covers,	" 8		Scales and weights	1 box	
			" " " large,	No. 1	
			Sheepskins, dressed,	" 1	6 doz.
FURNITURE, ETC.			Spoons, table,		No. 6
			Spatulas, 3 and 6 in.,	" 2	" 4
Basins, tin, small,	No. 2	No. 8	Tumblers, tin,		
" washhand,	" 3	" 8	Urinals, glass,	" 2	
Bed pans, self (shovel-shape),	" 1	" 4	Vials, assorted,	2 doz.	

Except the following articles, which will be carried, in the box in the ambulances, under the driver's seat:

Beef stock, 2 lb. cans,	no. 3	Spoons, table,	no. 6
Buckets, leather,	" 1	Tumblers, tin,	" 6
Kettles, camp,	" 1	Hard bread,	10 lbs.
Lantern and candle,	" 1		

" These boxes will be kept locked. The Surgeon in charge of the brigade will keep the keys, and, by weekly inspections, ascertain that each ambulance has its full supply. Whenever practicable, one ambulance will follow in the rear of the regiment on the march to transport the medicine chest, knapsacks, and any urgent cases of sickness or wounds. When the ambulance cannot accompany the regiment, one knapsack will be carried by an orderly with the command, and the medicine chest and remaining knapsacks will be placed with the hospital tent and other hospital furniture in the wagon allowed to each regiment for that purpose. The hard bread can always be obtained from the savings of the regimental hospital.

"Note.—*February* 2, 1863.—In future, in ordinary cases the amount 'on hand' of all articles for which requisition is made must be stated. Requisitions to fill up the brigade supply to the amount ordered to be kept on hand, will be made for such articles as are necessary for this purpose.

"(Signed)   JONA. LETTERMAN,
Medical Director."

To carry into effect the requirements of this circular, arrangements were made for one "army wagon" to be attached to each regiment exclusively for hospital purposes, and one army wagon to each brigade to carry supplies in bulk, which allowance was found ample. Before the adoption of this system, one and sometimes two wagons were required to transport the medical supplies of a regiment, another to carry the hospital tents, cooking utensils, baggage of Medical officers, etc., and were frequently diverted from their legitimate use. With this change in the mode of furnishing the Medical Department of a regiment, its medical and surgical supplies would not be lost, even if "military necessity" required the wagons for other purposes; as they were in such quantity and put up in such a manner as to be readily carried on a horse, the Surgeons had no difficulty in replenishing their supplies, the state of which was always known to the Surgeon-in-Chief of brigade, whose duty required him to check any waste, and, at the same time, to see that the supplies were constantly kept up. Supplies, in accordance with this change, were ordered from New York and Philadelphia, but did not arrive in time to furnish the Army completely before we left Maryland, and the equipment was continued at Warrenton and Falmouth until the requirements of the circular were fully carried into effect. Subsequent events demonstrated the superiority of this method of supplying the department. These instructions having been issued, my attention was given to the manner of treating the wounded on the field. As far as I knew, no system of field hospitals existed in any of our armies, and, convinced of the necessity of devising some measures by which the wounded would receive the best surgical aid which the Army afforded with the least delay, my thoughts

naturally turned to this most important subject. On
the field of battle, where confusion in the Medical
Department is most disastrous, it is most apt to occur,
and unless some arrangement be adopted by which
every Medical officer has his station pointed out and
his duties defined beforehand, and his accountability
strictly enforced, the wounded must suffer. To remedy the want which existed, I instituted the system
of field hospitals, as exhibited in the following circular:

"HEADQUARTERS, ARMY OF THE POTOMAC,
        Medical Director's Office, October 30, 1862.

"SIR: In order that the wounded may receive the
most prompt and efficient attention during and after
an engagement, and that the necessary operations may
be performed by the most skilful and responsible
Surgeons at the earliest moment, the following instructions are issued for the guidance of the Medical Staff
of this Army, and Medical Directors of Corps will
see that they are promptly carried into effect:

"Previous to an engagement there will be established in each Corps an hospital for each division, the
position of which will be selected by the Medical
Director of the Corps.

"The organization of the hospital will be as fol-
lows:

"1st. A Surgeon in charge, one Assistant-Surgeon,

to provide food and shelter, etc.; one Assistant-Surgeon, to keep the records.

"2d. Three Medical officers, to perform operations; three Medical officers, as assistants to each of these officers.

"3d. Additional Medical officers, hospital stewards, nurses of the division.

"The Surgeon in charge will have general superintendence, and be responsible to the Surgeon-in-Chief of the division for the proper administration of the hospital. The Surgeon-in-Chief of division will detail one Assistant-Surgeon, who will report to and be under the immediate orders of the Surgeon in charge, whose duties shall be to pitch the hospital tents and provide straw, fuel, water, blankets, etc., and, when houses are used, put them in proper order for the reception of wounded. This Assistant-Surgeon will, when the foregoing shall have been accomplished, at once organize a kitchen, using for this purpose the hospital mess chests and the kettles, tins, etc., in the ambulances. The supplies of beef stock and bread in the ambulances, and of arrowroot, tea, etc., in the hospital wagon, will enable him to prepare quickly a sufficient quantity of palatable and nourishing food. All the cooks, and such of the hospital stewards and nurses as may be necessary, will be placed under his orders for these purposes.

"He will detail another Assistant-Surgeon, whose duty it shall be to keep a complete record of every case brought to the hospital, giving the name, rank, company, and regiment, the seat and character of injury, the treatment, the operation, if any be performed, and the result, which will be transmitted to the Medical Director of the Corps, and by him sent to this office.

"This officer will also see to the proper interment of those who die, and that the grave is marked with a head-board, with the name, rank, company, and regiment legibly inscribed upon it.

"He will make out two "Tabular Statements of Wounded," which the Surgeon-in-Chief of division will transmit, within thirty-six hours after a battle, one to this office (by a special messenger, if necessary), and the other to the Medical Director of the Corps to which the hospital belongs.

"There will be selected from the division, by the Surgeon-in-Chief, under the direction of the Medical Director of the Corps, three Medical officers, who will be the operating staff of the hospital, upon whom will rest the immediate responsibility of the performance of all important operations. In all doubtful cases they will consult together, and a majority of them shall decide upon the expediency and character of the operation. These officers will be selected from the division without regard to rank, but *solely* on account of their known prudence, judgment, and skill. The Surgeon-in-Chief of the division is enjoined to be especially careful in the selection of these officers, choosing only those who have distinguished themselves for surgical skill, sound judgment, and conscientious regard for the highest interests of the wounded.

"There will be detailed three Medical officers to act as assistants to each one of these officers, who will report to him and act entirely under his direction. It is suggested that one of these assistants be selected to administer the anæsthetic. Each operating Surgeon will be provided with an excellent table from the hospital wagon, and, with the present organization for field hospitals, it is hoped that the confusion and the delay in performing the necessary operations so often existing after a battle, will be avoided, and all operations hereafter be *primary*.

"The remaining Medical officers of the division, except one to each regiment, will be ordered to the hospitals to act as dressers and assistants generally. Those who follow the regiments to the field will establish themselves, each one at a temporary depot, at such a distance or situation in the rear of his regiment as will insure safety to the wounded, where they will give such aid as is immediately required;

and they are here reminded that, whilst no personal consideration should interfere with their duty to the wounded, the grave responsibilities resting upon them render any unnecessary exposure improper.

The Surgeon-in-Chief of the division will exercise general supervision, under the Medical Director of the Corps, over the medical affairs in his division. He will see that the officers are faithful in the performance of their duties in the hospital and upon the field, and that by the Ambulance Corps, which has heretofore been so efficient, the wounded are removed from the field carefully and with despatch.

"Whenever his duties permit, he will give his professional services at the hospital—will order to the hospital, as soon as located, all the hospital wagons of the brigades, the hospital tents and furniture, and all the hospital stewards and nurses. He will notify the captain commanding the Ambulance Corps, or if this be impracticable, the first lieutenant commanding the division ambulances, of the location of the hospital.

"No Medical officer will leave the position to which he shall have been assigned without permission; and any officer so doing will be reported to the Medical Director of the Corps, who will report the facts to this office.

"The Medical Directors of Corps will apply to

their commanders on the eve of a battle, for the necessary guard and men for fatigue duty. This guard will be particularly careful that no stragglers be allowed about the hospitals, using the food and comforts prepared for the wounded. No wounded will be sent away from any of these hospitals without authority from this office.

" Previous to an engagement, a detail will be made, by Medical Directors of Corps, of a proper number of Medical officers, who will, should a retreat be found necessary, remain and take care of the wounded. This detail, Medical Directors will request the corps commanders to announce in orders.

" The skilful attention shown by the Medical officers of this Army, to the wounded upon the battlefields of South Mountain, Crampton's Gap, and Antietam, under trying circumstances, gives the assurance that, with this organization, the Medical Staff of the Army of the Potomac can with confidence be relied upon, under all emergencies, to take charge of wounded intrusted to its care.

" Very respectfully,

" Your obedient servant,

" (Signed)   JONA. LETTERMAN,

Medical Director."

It will be perceived that the ambulance system,

with that of supplies and of field hospitals, were
ordered as essential parts of that new organization
from which, I earnestly hoped, the wounded and sick
would receive more careful attendance and more skilful treatment. The Army crossed the Potomac into
Virginia in the latter part of October and early in
November, in the expectation of soon meeting the
enemy again. Our cavalry, being in the advance,
had daily skirmishes with that of the opposing forces,
and gave the department a few wounded to provide
for. Beyond this, nothing of interest, in a medical
point of view, took place during our very rapid
march through this portion of the State. I had
made all the arrangements that time permitted to
carry out the instructions contained in the system I
had established; and with the hearty coöperation
given me by the ablest Medical officers of the Army,
I felt, in the event of a battle, this Department would
be better able than ever, to discharge the duties
devolving upon it. General McClellan having been
relieved, General Burnside assumed command of the
Army at Warrenton, Virginia, on the 9th of November—on the 17th the Army left for Fredericksburg,
Virginia, and on the 19th arrived opposite that city.
It was generally believed that we could at once cross
the Rappahannock, and take possession of the city.
It soon became apparent that, should we make the

attempt, we would encounter a strong opposition. The great uncertainty that prevailed regarding our movements was not conducive to proper and well-directed exertion. I was busily employed in having my department well prepared, and ready for any emergency which might arise: to attain this end, my attention was principally directed to the instructions of the circulars of October 4th and October 30th, 1862, to see that they were clearly understood, and as fully carried out as was possible, previous to an engagement; that an extra amount of supplies was in the hands of the purveyor, and easily procured; that the Ambulance Corps should be established in all portions of the Army, and perfectly equipped. I directed Assistant-Surgeon Thomas McMillin, U. S. A., the Medical Purveyor, to leave Knoxville, Maryland, as soon as the Army had crossed into Virginia, and proceed with his supplies to Washington—there to await orders. Before we reached Warrenton he was ordered to that place, where he was busily engaged in fitting out officers, according to the requirements issued on the 4th of October; he was afterwards ordered to the depot at Aquia Creek, where ample supplies had been ordered from New York and elsewhere, which were rapidly issued. I may state here, that a sufficient number of "hospital wagons" could not be procured, nor was it ever in

5

my power to remedy the deficiency in this very important article, required by the circular.   In addition
to the regular supplies, large quantities of beef stock,
stimulants, and dressings of all kinds, milk, coffee,
tea, blankets, shirts, drawers, etc., etc., were procured,
and packed, ready to be sent at any moment to such
a point as I might direct.   The Medical Directors of
Corps were informed that these articles had been procured, and that, in the event of an engagement, they
would be brought to an easily accessible point—
where Medical officers could procure all they desired,
without any formal requisition, invoices, or receipts,
but simply on the written request of the officer.   The
details required by the circular of October 30th
were made, blanks distributed, and all possible steps
taken to carry the provisions of that order into effect.
The Ambulance Corps throughout the Army was
carefully examined—horses, harness, stretchers, lanterns, etc., etc., were procured, and officers assigned and
men detailed to complete and render effective this
organization.   Five hundred extra hospital tents
were ordered, at my request, by Colonel (now Major-
General) Ingalls, the Chief Quartermaster, and kept
at the depot, ready to be used when I required
them.   I now felt that when my department should
be called upon, every thing had been done, in the
inauguration of the new system, to make it equal to

the demands which might be made upon it. On the 11th of December the pontoon bridges were ready to be thrown over the Rappahannock. The positions of the batteries had been selected, and the guns placed in position on the north bank of that river. I did not anticipate many casualties among the artillerists, and therefore directed only three locations to be selected as hospitals for all the wounded. These instructions were carried out, and my anticipations regarding the number of wounded were realized. The nature of the impending battle was somewhat peculiar, as far as it involved the Medical Department. In the attempt to lay the bridges over the river in front of the city, determined opposition was to be expected from the enemy; and should the bridges be constructed, the troops would doubtless cross under the fire of the enemy's guns which were planted on the heights beyond, and commanded the bridges, and the streets leading from them into the city. In this case, accommodations must be prepared, on the north side of the river, for a large number of wounded. Should we succeed in crossing, and in taking possession of the city, without opposition, in all probability the troops would be immediately pushed on, and the attempt made to dislodge the enemy from the heights, which gave him complete control of the city. In this case, hospitals must be

established in Fredericksburg, as soon as the troops
entered it; and yet it was equally necessary, even if
we crossed without molestation—if we failed in carrying the heights—that the wounded should be removed, at a moment's notice, to the north side of the
river, beyond reach of the hostile guns.   Preparations
were made for these contingencies—the hospitals
were formed by divisions, as the order required; "the
surgeons were at their · posts ready for duty, with
their attendants, nurses, food, medicines, and all that
the wounded might need"*—and all the hospitals were in such order as to give "the most pleasing assurance of the efficiency to meet the emergencies of the approaching engagement." † On the
morning of December 11th the attempt was
made to throw the bridges over the river; the
artillery opened upon the enemy's works beyond the
city, and upon that portion of it which skirted the
river, whence the riflemen of the opposing forces were
pouring a deadly fire upon the engineers engaged in
constructing these bridges.   As the day advanced
our fire became more terrific, and, late in the afternoon, the enemy, few in number, were driven from
the cellars and other places of concealment along the
bank of the river.   Three bridges were then speedily

---

* Report of Surgeon O'Connell, Medical Director of the Ninth Corps.
† Report of Surgeon O'Leary, Medical Director of the Sixth Corps.

thrown over on our right. Two bridges were constructed on our left wing, where much less opposition was encountered.

No serious attempt was made after this to prevent the crossing of the troops, which took place on the evening of the 11th and the following day. The few wounded were speedily and properly attended. In examining that portion of the city in our possession (the enemy still occupying that part of it farthest from the river), on the 12th, to ascertain its capacities for hospital purposes, I was struck by the desolation everywhere visible. The court-house, several churches, and such other buildings as were suitable, were selected by Dr. Dougherty, the Medical Director of the Right Grand Division, and Dr. Moore, the Medical Director of the Centre Grand Division, and the Medical Directors of the Corps engaged—a sufficient number of hospital wagons sent over—and so earnestly did the Medical officers enter upon the discharge of their duties, that the hospitals were in readiness with surgeons, attendants, guards, instruments, dressings, stimulants, food, candles, etc., etc., before the action began. The wounded on the north ride of the river were left in charge of a sufficient number of Medical officers and attendants, with plenty of medical and surgical supplies, and food. All the hospitals were left standing, and hospital tents

were placed in the depot opposite Fredericksburg, ready to be pitched, should we require
them.

The left wing of the Army crossed on the same
days as the right. Here, also, hospitals were established on the north side of the river and on the south
bank—the most sheltered locations were chosen for
them; it was found impossible to place them beyond
the range of the enemy's guns. Owing to the nature
of the action on this part of the field, the Medical
officers were more able to carry out the hospital organization. In the Sixth Corps " each hospital had
three operating tables, with the requisite number of
Surgeons and attendants assigned to them separately.
Instruments, dressings, and all the appliances necessary,
were arranged with order, precision, and convenience
rarely excelled in regular hospitals. Each Surgeon
knew his proper place, and devoted himself to the
duty pertaining to it with a zeal and fidelity worthy
of the highest commendation. I only give you the
testimony of commanding officers, as well as Medical
officers, when I state to you that the preparations here
made in a very short time presented the completeness
in detail belonging to long-established hospitals, rather
than to extemporized field hospitals; and were I to
explain in full this organization, I would only be re-

peating the instructions laid down in the circular, to
which we strictly adhered." *

The Medical officers detailed to accompany the
troops into action, were directed to establish themselves in the most accessible and sheltered places in
rear of their respective brigades, where the wounded
would be carried by the stretcher-bearers, who were
ordered to keep themselves constantly informed of
the position of these officers. Here the wound d
would receive such attendance as was imperatively
required, after which they would be conveyed to their
division hospitals by the ambulances. The fighting
on the right would be only a short distance from the
city, and the position of the enemy would prevent the
use of the ambulances during the action. The hospitals in the city were made known to the Medical
officers accompanying the troops and to the stretcher-
bearers of the division. Before the action began, the
extra supplies heretofore mentioned were brought to
the depot near Fredericksburg by the Medical Purveyor, who, in accordance with my wishes, came to
see the field of operations, that he might the better
execute any orders he might receive in reference to
supplies when he returned to Aquia Creek. The
Medical Directors were informed where these supplies
were deposited, and were directed to have the infor-

* Report of Surgeon O'Leary, Medical Director of the Sixth Corps.

mation conveyed to all their subordinate officers. The battle began on the morning of the 13th December, and lasted until dark. The bearing of the troops on the right was admirable. From the headquarters of General Burnside they could be seen advancing and driven back by the murderous fire of the enemy. Again and again they re-formed and pressed forward over the wounded, the dying, and the dead, close to fortifications, rifle-pits, and stone walls, behind which the foe was concealed; their gallantry and persever-ance, under circumstances so disheartening, challeng-ing the admiration of all who watched with intense anxiety the progress of the battle. Throughout the day the wounded were rapidly brought in, and were promptly and efficiently treated. As night closed in, the firing slackened, and shortly after ceased. The ambulances, which could not be used while the battle lasted, were now employed' in gathering in the wounded, numbers of whom then remained upon the field. The night was very dark, and the officers and men of this corps experienced great difficulty in find-ing the objects of their search. They could not use their lanterns, as the glimmer of a candle invariably called forth a shot from a sharpshooting picket. They were obliged to grope their way, and search for their wounded comrades, who lay on the field, covered by the fire of the enemy's musketry, which made it hazardous for the wounded, or those seeking them, to move over that sanguinary ground, even when protected by the darkness. The officers and men of this corps persevered so well, notwithstanding the difficulties which beset them, that before dawn all the wounded, who were not beyond our lines, were taken to the hospitals prepared for them in the rear. The duties of Medical officers, unlike those of the line, did not cease with the close of the day, but continued throughout the night. The hospitals, although located in the most sheltered parts of the city, were not free from danger after dark. Every light reminded the officers of the vicinity of the enemy, and blankets were placed over the windows, and each aperture closed to conceal the lights, every appearance of which drew a shot from the hostile guns planted on the heights beyond. During the day several hospitals were struck by shot and shell from these guns, but fortunately no one was injured. The preparations were found ample and judicious, and the wounded were speedily brought in from the field and skilfully attended.

Regarding the operations of this department on the left wing, it is only necessary to remark that orders given before the battle were strictly obeyed by the Medical officers and their assistants, each one of whom endeavored, with praiseworthy emulation, to

surpass the other in devotion to the wounded. Promptness and order characterized the action of the Ambulance Corps on this exciting day. So well was its
duty performed, that not a wounded man was left
upon the field when darkness put an end to the conflict. On the 14th December the troops remained on
the field, the Surgeons continued their labors, and, on
the evening of that day, comparatively few important
operations remained to be performed. On the 15th,
in compliance with orders of the Commanding General given late on the preceding night, the wounded
were removed to the north side of the river. The
hospitals were ready, and the propriety of leaving
them standing was now apparent. Before six o'clock
in the evening all the wounded were safely transported to these hospitals, where every thing was prepared for their reception. Some delay occurred early
in the day in removing the wounded from the city, in
consequence of an order having been misunderstood.
This was soon remedied, and long trains of ambulances might be seen crossing the river, halting in the
city to receive the sufferers, then wending their way
over the upper bridge to the hospitals of their respective divisions. After the last train had left, the
city was thoroughly examined by my direction to
prevent any wounded man being left. During the
night of the 13th the wounded of the First Corps

were removed to their respective division hospitals on
the north bank of the river. The wounded of the
Sixth Corps were removed on the 14th, by one o'clock
in the afternoon, to the hospitals prepared for them
before the battle. A portion only of the ambulances
of this Corps were engaged in this duty, the remainder
being held in readiness in the event of a renewal of
the battle which might occur at any moment. The
movements of this wing of the Army requiring the
removal of these hospitals still farther to the rear, the
wounded were safely and comfortably lodged during
the night. About five thousand were removed to the
north side of the river. The transportation of this
number, in the short time allowed, without accident
and without confusion, under the belief that the
enemy would open his guns upon our troops, who
filled the city, was a sufficient test of the efficacy of
the system; and the manner in which it was carried
out reflected the highest credit upon the officers in
charge, and afforded great satisfaction to the Generals
in command.

The following tables exhibit the grand divisions
and corps and the number of regiments, with their
strength, the number of killed, wounded, and missing,
the Surgeons-in-Chief of division, and the number of
Medical officers present in this battle:

RIGHT GRAND DIVISION.

Major-General SUMNER, Commanding.

Surgeon A. N. DOUGHERTY, U. S. Vol., *Medical Director.*

SECOND CORPS.

Major-General COUCH, Commanding.

Surgeon J. H. TAYLOR, U. S. Vol., *Medical Director.*

DIVISIONS.	Surgeons-in-Chief.	No. of Regiments engaged.	Mean strength for duty on the day of the battle.	No. of wounded according to regim'l reports	No. of killed accord to regiment'l reports.	Missing.	No. of Medical officers present.
1st Division,	D. H. Houston...	17	5491	1543	238	181	31
2d "	W. H. Morton..	15	6355	625	122	26	30
3d "	J. Scott.......	14	5352	895	110	144	23
		46	17,198	3063	470	351	84

NINTH CORPS.

Brigadier-General WILCOX, Commanding.

Surgeon P. A. O'CONNELL, 22d Mass., *Medical Director.*

DIVISIONS.	Surgeons-in-Chief.	No. of Regiments engaged.	Mean strength for duty on the day of the battle.	No. of wounded according to regim'l reports	No. of killed accord to regiment'l reports.	Missing.	No. of Medical officers present.
1st Division,	H. Hovet......	12	5771	28	1	1	30
2d "	A. T. Watson...	11	5272	779	95	51	19
3d "	M. Storrs......	12	6593	189	22	53	25
		35	17,636	996	118	105	74

CENTRE GRAND DIVISION.

Major-General HOOKER, Commanding.

Surgeon JOHN MOORE, U. S. A., *Medical Director.*

THIRD CORPS.

Brigadier-General STONEMAN, Commanding.

Surgeon G. L. PANCOAST, U. S. Vol., *Medical Director.*

DIVISIONS.	Surgeons-in-Chief.	No. of Regiments engaged.	Mean strength for duty on the day of the battle.	No. of wounded according to regim'l reports.	No. of killed according to regiment'l reports.	Missing.	No. of Medical officers present.
1st Division,	O. Everett......	17	7582	585	114	142	35
2d "	Thomas Sim....	17	7721	75	11	6	42
3d " .	J. S. Jamison ..	9	4183	96	18	30	19
		43	19,486	756	143	178	96

FIFTH CORPS.

Brigadier-General BUTTERFIELD, Commanding.

Assistant-Surgeon R. O. CRAIG, U. S. A., *Medical Director.*

DIVISIONS.	Surgeons-in-Chief	No. of Regiments engaged.	Mean strength for duty on the day of the battle.	No. of wounded according to regim'l reports.	No. of killed according to regiment'l reports.	Missing.	No. of Med. officers present.
1st Division,	J. Owen.	18	7089	772	72	93	35
2d "	W. R. Ramsey..	15	5571	157	18	22	16
3d "	J. D. Knight...	8	3753	760	109	137	20
		41	16,413	1689	199	252	71

LEFT GRAND DIVISION.

Major-General FRANKLIN, Commanding.

FIRST CORPS.

Major-General REYNOLDS, Commanding.

Surgeon J. THEO. HEARD, U. S. Vol., *Medical Director*.

DIVISIONS.	Surgeons-in-Chief.	No. of Regiments engaged.	Mean strength for duty on the day of the battle.	No. of wounded according to regim'l reports	No. of killed accord. to regiment'l reports.	Missing.	No. of Med. officers present.
1st Division,	E. Shippen.....	17	5071	138	28	45	38
2d "	C. J. Nordquist..	14	4712	989	146	96	80
3d "	L. W. Read....	15	6097	1135	183	441	29
		46	15,880	2262	357	582	97

SIXTH CORPS.

Major-General SMITH, Commanding.

Surgeon CHARLES O'LEARY, U. S. Vol., *Medical Director*.

DIVISIONS.	Surgeons-in-Chief.	No. of Regiments engaged.	Mean strength for duty on the day of the battle.	No. of wounded according to regim'l reports	No. of killed accord. to regiment'l reports.	Missing.	No. of Med. officers present.
1st Division,	E. F. Taylor.....	14	7351	121	25	54	33
2d "	S. J. Allen......	14	8144	139	23	—	30
3d "	S. A. Holman...	15	7344	34	4	8	34
		43	22,839	294	52	62	97

RECAPITULATION.

ARMY OF THE POTOMAC.	No. of Regiments engaged.	Mean strength for duty on the day of the battle.	No. of wounded according to regimental reports.	No. killed according to regimental reports.	No. missing according to regimental reports.	Total killed, wounded, and missing, acc'g to regimental reports.
	254	109,452	9,060	1,339	1,530	11,929

The following tables, exhibiting the number of wounded, the seat of injury, etc., etc., were compiled from the "lists of wounded" sent to me from the different hospitals, in which the name of every man was recorded. I am indebted to Assistant-Surgeon Warren Webster, U. S. A., for them, and I believe them to be strictly accurate.

WOUNDED IN THE SECOND CORPS.

REGION.	Number of wounded.	CHARACTER OF MISSILE.				OPERATIONS.				REMARKS.
		Cannon ball.	Shell.	Bullet.	Unclassified.	Amputations.	Resections.	Other operations.	Total.	
Head,...........	250	14	37	51	148					It is mentioned in 30 instances only, that chloroform was administered. No deaths from its use.
Neck,..........	39		7	15	17					
Chest, ...	91		12	38	41					
Abdomen, ...	37	1	8	8	20					
Side,...........	85				85					
Back and spine, ..	58	2	17	11	28					
Hips and genitals,	124	5	17	29	73					
Shoulder,........	194	7	26	68	93	2			2	
Arm, ...	326	5	39	96	186	39	3	2	44	
Forearm and hand,	269	4	29	82	154	4			4	
Thigh, ...	188	7	20	58	103	23			23	
Knee,...........	46				46	3	1		4	
Leg, ...	420	15	61	113	231	27	2	1	30	
Ankle, ...	36				36					
Foot, ...	136	6	17	96	17	4			4	
Fingers, ...	11				11	7			7	
Toes, ...										
Unclassified, ...	255				255	4			4	
Total,......	2565	66	290	665	1544	113	6	3	122	

WOUNDED IN THE NINTH CORPS.

REGION.	Number of wounded.	CHARACTER OF MISSILE.				OPERATIONS.				REMARKS.
		Cannon-ball.	Shell.	Bullet.	Unclassified.	Amputations.	Resections.	Other operations.	Total.	
Head,..........	67		25	31	11					
Neck,..........	4		1	2	1					
Chest, ...	18		6	12						
Abdomen, ...	6		1	5				2	2	
Side,..........	13				13					
Back and spine ..	28		4	17	7					
Hips and genitals,	26		9	17				1	1	
Shoulders, ...	42		8	28	6	1	2		3	
Arm, ...	66		25	41		14	1	1	16	
Forearm and hand,	52		12	31	9	15	1		16	
Thigh, ...	45		13	32		8		1	9	
Knee,..........	12		2		10					
Leg,...........	77	6	14	57		26	1	5	32	
Ankle, ...	13				13	1			1	
Foot, ...	27	1	3	23		2			2	
Fingers, ...	13				13	5			5	
Toes, ...										
Unclassified, ...	25				25					
Total,.....	534	7	123	296	108	72	5	10	87	It is mentioned that chloroform was administered in 123 cases. No deaths from its use.

WOUNDED IN THE THIRD CORPS.

REGION.	Number of wounded.	CHARACTER OF MISSILE.				OPERATIONS.				REMARKS.
		Cannon-ball.	Shell.	Bullet.	Unclassified.	Amputations.	Resections.	Other operations.	Total.	
Head,..........	65		8	57				1	1	It is mentioned that chloroform was administered in 58 cases. No deaths resulted from its use.
Neck,..........	16		1	12	3					
Chest, ...	22		5	17						
Abdomen, ...	14		5	9						
Side,...........	1				1					
Back and spine, ..	27		6	14	7					
Hips and genitals,	38		4	21	13					
Shoulders,......	37		2	32	3	1	1		2	
Arm, ?.........	73		4	57	12	10	2		12	
Forearm and hand.	79		5	74		10	3		13	
Thigh, ...	84		4	80		11			11	
Knee,..........	26				26	5			5	
Leg,...........	115		13	102		16		1	17	
Ankle, ...	14				14	1			1	
Foot, ...	23		2	20	1	1	1	1	3	
Fingers,........	27				27	23			23	
Toes, ...	1				1					
Unclassified......	10				10					
Total,.....	672		59	495	118	78	7	3	88	

6

WOUNDED IN THE FIFTH CORPS.

REGION.	Number of wounded.	CHARACTER OF MISSILE.				OPERATIONS.				REMARKS.
		Cannon-ball.	Shell.	Bullet.	Unclassified.	Amputations.	Resections.	Other operations.	Total.	
Head,............	130		1	51	78					It is stated that chloroform was only administered in 15 cases. No deaths resulted from its use.
Neck,...........	14			12	2					
Chest, ...	51			33	18					
Abdomen, ...	19			19						
Side,............	39				39					
Back and spine, ..	42			22	20					
Hips and genitals,	79		1	44	34					
Shoulder,........	108			71	37					
Arm, ...	117		3	68	46					
Forearm and hand,	114		1	71	42					
Thigh, ...	106		4	52	50	3			3	
Knee,...........	24				24	2			2	
Leg, ...	138		2	65	71	17			17	
Ankle, ...	20				20					
Foot, ...	58			32	26	1			1	
Fingers, ...	29				29	19			19	
Toes, ...	2				2					
Unclassified, ...	59				59					
Total,......	1149		12	540	597	42			42	

WOUNDED IN THE FIRST CORPS.

REGION.	Number of wounded.	CHARACTER OF MISSILE.				OPERATIONS.				REMARKS.
		Cannon-ball.	Shell.	Bullet.	Unclassified.	Amputations.	Resections.	Other operations.	Total.	
Head, ...	182	1	29	122	30					
Neck, ...	23			21	2					
Chest, ...	132	1	19	108	4					
Abdomen, ...	34	1	7	25	1					
Side, ...	5				5					Chloroform was administered in 237 cases, with no ill effects.
Back and spine, . .	47		19	21	7					
Hips and genitals,	101	2	16	39	44					
Shoulders, ...	107		21	80	6	1	1	1	3	
Arm, ...	211	1	30	162	18	24	4		28	
Forearm and hand,	150		29	111	10	12	2		14	
Thigh, ...	226		28	187	11	19			19	
Knee, ...	3				3	28	1	1	30	
Leg, ...	447	5	48	373	21	6		3	9	
Ankle, ...	5				5	1				
Foot, ...	89	1	34	46	8	18			18	
Fingers, ...	25				25	4			4	
Toes, ...	6				6		2		2	
Unclassified, ...	3				3					
Total, ...	1796	12	280	1295	209	112	10	5	127	

WOUNDED IN THE SIXTH CORPS.

REGION.	Number of wounded.	CHARACTER OF MISSILE.				OPERATIONS.				REMARKS.
		Cannon-ball.	Shell.	Bullet.	Unclassified.	Amputations.	Resections.	Other operations.	Total.	
Head,..........	48		14	27	7				1	
Neck,..........	7		1	5	1					
Chest, ...	9		1	8						
Abdomen, ...	5		2	3						
Side,..........	9			9						
Back and spine, ..	10		2	8						
Hips and genitals,	15		1	10	4					The administration of chloroform is only mentioned in 25 instances. No deaths reported from its use.
Shoulders,.......	21	1		20						
Arm, ...	43		8	28	7	5			5	
Forearm and hand.	43		11	28	4	2		1	3	
Thigh, ...	36		1	32	3	7			7	
Knee,..........	11				11	2			2	
Leg,..........	35		3	28	4	6			6	
Ankle, ...	4				4	1			1	
Foot, ...	17		3	12	2	6			6	
Fingers, ...	4				4	5			5	
....										
Unclassified......	15				15					
Total,.....	332	1	47	218	66	34		1	35	

TOTAL WOUNDED OF THE ENGINEER CORPS AND ARTILLERY
RESERVE.

REGION.	Number of wounded.	CHARACTER OF MISSILE.				OPERATIONS.				REMARKS.
		Cannon-ball.	Shell.	Bullet.	Unclassified.	Amputations.	Resections.	Other operations.	Total.	
Head,..........	2				2					The administration of chloroform is not mentioned.
Neck,..........	3				3					
Chest, ...	2				2					
Abdomen, ...	2				2					
Side,...........										
Back and spine, ..	2			1	1					
Hips and genitals,	8			1	2					
Shoulder,........	1			1						
Arm, ...	4			2	2					
Forearm and hand,	11			1	10					
Thigh, ...	10				10	2			2	
Knee,..........	1				1					
Leg, ...	5			3	2					
Ankle, ...	2				2					
Foot, ...	3			1	2					
Fingers, ...	1				1					
Toes, ...										
Unclassified, ...										
Total,.....	52			10	42	2			2	

WOUNDED IN THE FIRST CORPS.

REGION.	Number of wounded.	CHARACTER OF MISSILE.				OPERATIONS.				REMARKS.
		Cannon-ball.	Shell.	Bullet.	Unclassified.	Amputations.	Resections.	Other operations.	Total.	
Head,...........	744	15	114	339	276			1	1	The administration of chloroform is only mentioned in 498 instances. No fatal results from its use.
Neck,...........	106		10	67	29					
Chest, ...	325	1	43	216	65					
Abdomen, ...	117	2	23	69	23			2	2	
Side,...........	152			9	143					
Back and spine, ..	214	2	48	94	70					
Hips and genitals,	386	7	48	161	170			1	1	
Shoulders, ...	510	8	57	300	145	5	4	1	10	
Arm, ...	840	6	109	454	271	92	10	3	105	
Forearm and hand,	718	4	87	398	229	43	6	1	50	Chloroform was used very freely, and no operation of any consequence was performed without it. The number of instances mentioned give no just idea of its use.
Thigh, ...	695	7	70	441	177	73		1	74	
Knee,...........	123		2		121	40	2	1	43	
Leg,............	1237	26	141	741	329	98	3	10	111	
Ankle, ...	94				94	21			21	
Foot, ...	353	8	59	230	56	18	1	1	20	
Fingers, ...	110				110	59	2		61	
Toes, ...	9				9					
Unclassified, ...	367				367	4			4	
Total,.....	7100	86	811	3519	2684	453	28	22	503	

Having been directed to send these wounded to the General Hospitals in Washington, I began their removal on the 16th of December, and continued it from time to time, until the 26th of that month, when the last were sent away. I was very anxious to pursue the same course toward the seriously wounded in this battle, as I did with similar cases in the battle of Antietam. Many lives had been saved by the establishment of the Antietam hospital, and I felt convinced that such an institution would again produce the same happy effect. The tent hospitals were fitted up comfortably, with all the necessary appliances, and the Medical officers were taking the deepest interest in their patients. I represented the matter to the Commanding General, but he desired me to send them away without any unnecessary delay. Soon after the action, the slightly wounded were sent in charge of Medical officers to Aquia Creek depot, by railroad, and thence by steamers to Washington. In the removal of the serious cases, the floors of the cars were covered with hay, upon which mattresses, beds, and bed-sacks filled with hay were placed, and the patients carefully taken from the hospitals, and put in the cars; in the very serious cases the sufferers were not removed from the mattresses upon which they lay in the hospitals, but were carried by hand to the cars, whence they were removed in like manner

to the transports, remaining undisturbed upon their
beds until they reached Washington. A Medical
officer, with an attendant, and instruments, stimulants, and dressings, was in each car, and, when
necessary, he accompanied his patients to Washington. Every care was taken of these men, who in numerous instances expressed with much feeling their
gratitude for the kindness and attention of the Medical officers who had done so much to make their
transportation comfortable. I never saw wounded
men so carefully removed, and I can safely say that
no more suffering was occasioned than the severity
of the wounds necessarily entailed. While the battle
was in progress, and after it was over, nearly one
thousand men (no one of whom had a wound of any
consequence, and many were uninjured) jumped in
the cars, and climbed on the top, at the depot near
Fredericksburg, and went to Aquia Creek, twelve
miles distant, where they knew no hospitals were
established. Before the battle, strict orders had, at
my request, been given to the guard at this depot, to
allow no wounded to get on the cars; but unfortunately the guard was worthless, and permitted these
men to go, as fast as steam could carry them, out of
reach of the hospitals which they knew had been prepared for accommodation. These are the men who in
battle run to the rear, beyond even the sound of the

enemy's guns, and complain of the Surgeons, whom they sedulously avoid, lest their wounds should be found so trifling as not to prevent them from participating in the fight. These are the cowardly stragglers who abandon their colors on the field of battle for the slightest injury (often self-inflicted), and raise a clamor which, unhappily, too many are found to echo. How different those, whether slightly or seriously wounded, who have borne the burden and heat of the day!—rarely do they complain of want of care; on the contrary, expressions of thankfulness often escape their lips for the attention bestowed upon them.

The following table, furnished me by the Medical Purveyor, shows the extra supplies brought to the front. These were ready for issue before they were wanted, and were kept at the depot near the field, until no more were required. The Medical Directors of Corps, without exception, reported that all their hospitals were fully supplied with every thing necessary for the proper care and treatment of the wounded.

Table of Extra Amounts of Supplies at the Battle of Fredericksburg, Va.

ARTICLES.		Forwarded.	Issued.	Returned.	ARTICLES.		Forwarded.	Issued.	Returned.
Cerat simpl.,	lbs.	100	50	50	Field tourniquets,	No.	24	14	10
Chloroform,	"	200	44	156	Blankets,	"	5000	3775	1225
Emplast, adhes.,	yds.	400	300	100	Bed-sacks,	"	1000	790	210
" icthyocol.,	"	400	200	200	Muslin,	yds.	125	105	20
Magnes. sulph.,	lbs.	75	60	15	Pins,	papers	37	37	—
Morphia,	drs.	200	104	96	Surgeons' silk,	oz.	25	12	13
Ferri persulph.,	oz.	200	153	47	Sponge,	lbs.	50	45	5
" " liq.,	"	75	3	72	Oakum,	"	50	50	—
Opii pulv.,	lbs.	25	11	14	Bandages,	doz.	1000	965	35
" pillulæ,	doz.	400	400	—	Shirts,	No.	2000	1400	600
Pil. cathar. comp.,	"	300	292	8	Socks (pairs),	"	2000	1400	600
" opii et camph.,	"	50	45	5	Drawers,	"	1000	400	600
Brandy,	bot.	1800	1800	—	Camp-Kettles,	"	500	321	179
Whiskey,	"	4200	3600	600	Tin cups,	"	500	294	206
Tea,	lbs.	150	133	17	Knives,	"	2000	1922	78
Concentr'd ex. beef,	"	4484	4484	—	Forks,	"	2000	1922	78
Condensed milk,	"	800	720	80	Tin plates,	"	1500	1371	129
Ex. coffee, sugar and milk,	gals.	45	25	20	Spoons,	"	2500	1500	1000
					Tin tumblers,	"	500	292	208
Candles, sperm,	lbs.	50	30	20	Leather buckets,	"	100	90	10
Gener'l operat. cases,	No.	8	7	1	Stretchers,	"	300	260	40
Pocket cases,	"	11	11	—					

In this action we lost another highly esteemed Medical officer, Surgeon S. F. Haven, Fifteenth Massachusetts, who was killed by a shell, while advancing with his regiment to meet the enemy. Soon after the battle the Army was visited by Surgeon-General Hammond and the Congressional Committee on the Conduct of the War, who, after examining the hospitals, expressed their entire satisfaction with the administration of the Medical Department.

The troops returned to their former encampments, depressed by the defeat they had sustained. The

... of the Army was very much impaired, and ... might soon be called upon to meet the same ... it became all officers to use their utmost ... to encourage and arouse their men to a ... fighting tone. The care bestowed upon the ... in this engagement exerted a very benefi... influence upon the morale of the troops; for they ... if men did fall in a battle from which we ... only the bitter fruits of defeat, the Medical ... ment had become more able than before to ... important duty. There was no department ... labored more diligently to obviate the evil ... the late disaster. After every engagement, ... the issue, every portion of an army is more ... disorganized, and in no one is the effect more ... felt than in the Medical Department. After ... wounded had been sent to Washington, I was ... in perfecting the details of the organization ... I had instituted in the previous autumn, carry... measures for improving the health of the ... such as those regarding the location and ... of the camps, the food, cooking, and police of ... men; the reëstablishment of regimental hospi... etc., etc. We were now in the midst of winter, ... in this latitude is exceedingly inclement, and ... uncertain whether the troops would remain ... ary, and make themselves as comfortable as their surroundings would permit, or whether they would again be called upon to try the strength of the enemy. In the latter event, it was impossible to conjecture when or where this would be done. It is very difficult to labor in such a fog of uncertainty; nevertheless this Department was in a short time fully prepared to meet any emergency. This gratifying result was, in a great degree, owing to the manly, self-reliant feeling which pervaded the Medical Staff; —these officers deeply felt that proper organization had made their labors more valuable than ever before, and that their department was increasing in usefulness after every battle. Stimulated by the worthy pride of having succeeded so well in discharging the duties which devolved upon them at Fredericksburg, the Medical officers were conscious of their ability to accomplish still more in future. A Medical Board, consisting of Surgeons Suckley and Pineo, U. S. Volunteers, and Assistant-Surgeon Thomson, U. S. A., had been ordered in October, at my request, for the examination of Medical officers, whose professional qualifications were doubted. The proceedings of this Board were much interrupted by the movements of the Army shortly after its organization. Seventeen officers were, however, examined, three of whom were found competent and fourteen found incompetent to discharge the duties for which they had been com-

missioned. Careless and incompetent practitioners
were gradually weeded out by the action of similar
Boards, which were convened, from time to time, for
such investigations. On the 20th of January, 1863,
General Burnside ordered a forward movement. The
greater portion of the Army left its encampments,
with the view of turning the left flank of the enemy,
who lay on the south side of the Rappahannock. During the night following the marching of the troops
a very heavy rain fell; the mud became so deep, and
the low grounds along the river so covered with water,
as effectually to prevent the progress of the troops.
The delay consequent upon the state of the weather
made the design of the Commanding General evident to . the enemy, even if he were not already
aware of it, and the troops were ordered to return
to the camps which they had previously occupied.
Before this movement the most suitable site had been
selected near Aquia Creek depot, where hospitals
were established for the accommodation of the sick,
to break up the custom of sending great numbers of
men to General Hospitals on the eve of a march.
Upon the return of the troops to their encampments
these hospitals were broken up, the seriously ill sent
to Washington, and the remainder to the regimental
hospitals, which were reëstablished. In each corps
division hospitals, were formed, in accordance with

the instructions contained in my circular of October 30, 1862, as far as they were applicable to such cases, for taking care of such sick as could not be properly treated in regimental hospitals, and enabling Medical officers to become familiar with the manner in which such hospitals should be conducted. None were formed, however, in the Third Division of the Sixth Corps, under Surgeon Holman, the sick being amply provided for in the regimental hospitals. In the middle of January, the sickness in this Army, which then numbered nearly two hundred thousand men, was a little over eight per cent. When we consider the season of the year, the number of raw troops just added to the Army (fifty-six regiments), and the utterly inadequate protection afforded by the shelter tent, this percentage was not excessive. Leaving out the new regiments, the ratio was about five per cent. Venereal disease prevailed to a great degree among the newly arrived troops, among whom were also found numerous cases of hernia. On the 9th of January I directed the establishment of an hospital in Washington, exclusively for the treatment of these diseases. I wished more care bestowed upon such cases, and hoped the result of the treatment would be valuable to science, and more easily obtained than from the scattered records of the various hospitals throughout the country. The movement of the

Army, in anticipation of a battle, prevented me from giving further attention to the subject at this time, and in February a new department was created, including Washington, the commander of which was independent of the Commanding General of the Army of the Potomac; the hospitals in Washington, consequently, passed from my control, and my power to carry out this project ceased. I am unable to say whether an hospital of this kind was established, but I am still convinced of the propriety of the measure. The "List of Wounded" and "Tabular Statements" required to be sent to the Medical Director's office, were not as complete as I desired. I carefully revised them, and issued new forms, copies of which, and of the weekly reports of sick, will be found in the Appendix.

It was impossible, even with the aid of the Assistant Medical Director, Dr. Clements, U. S. A., in managing the Medical Department of so large an army, properly to inspect it. At my request, Assistant-Surgeon Warren Webster, U. S. A., was appointed Medical Inspector for the Army at large. The Medical Directors were held responsible, under general instructions, for the management of their Corps, and their duties were too onerous to allow them to give that minute attention to their departments, and to exercise that complete supervision of their officers,

which their position required. Early in January I
instituted a system of inspections, instructing each
Medical Director to appoint in his corps a Medical
Inspector, and, on the 9th of February, I issued the
following instructions for their guidance. (The form
referred to will be found in the Appendix:)

"HEADQUARTERS, ARMY OF THE POTOMAC,   ⎫
    Medical Director's Office, February 9, 1863. ⎬

"DOCTOR: Enclosed I send you a form of inspection
report, which I wish used in your Corps. This report
will be made monthly, and sent to this office within
three days after the close of the month during which
the inspection was made. You will also please require your Inspector to make to you a report in the
same form each week of the regiments and batteries
inspected. The main points to which it is thought
advisable to direct your attention, are sufficiently indicated by the headings, and no deviation from the
form will be made. Should, however, you or your
Inspector deem it of value to the service, or of interest to science, to make special observations or reports, not indicated by this form, they will be received
with favor. In forwarding this report, you will accompany it with a written report upon the general
sanitary condition of the troops, the attention of
Medical officers to their duties, and whatever in any

way affects the health of the men intrusted to your care,
or may be of value in rendering the Medical Department of your Corps more efficient, and you are desired
to communicate freely and unreservedly with me on
this subject. You will also, in this latter report, em-
body a history of the Corps sufficiently in detail to
give a clear knowledge of all its operations during the
month, that directly or indirectly bear upon the Medical Department, so that there may be in this office a
full medical history of the Corps under your charge.
It cannot be too strongly impressed upon your attention that the object of these inspections is to secure
reliable information as to the actual condition of the
Medical Department of this Army, and to bring to
notice all errors, neglects, deficiencies, and wants of
every kind; to bring to notice also the cases of
prompt and intelligent attention to duty, and of
earnest endeavor to promote the best interests of the
service; to bring to light the good as well as the bad.
In order to render these inspections of service, you are
especially desired to apply at once the proper remedy
for any evils that may exist, as soon as they are
brought to your notice, and no consideration must
deter you from acting fearlessly and without delay.
Inspections can only be of service when the errors
and wants which they bring to light are remedied upon
the spot. Should it be beyond your power to act

7

with the assistance of your commander, you will please report promptly the facts to this office. You will please require your Inspector to make special inspections, as often as you may deem necessary, to ascertain if your orders are carried out, and also direct him to instruct Medical officers in the proper mode of performing their duties, and particularly to impress upon them that the duties of Medical officers are not confined to prescribing drugs, but that it is also their duty, and one which is of the highest importance, to preserve the health of those who are well. This is a subject of the deepest interest, and Medical officers will be specially instructed upon this point, and directed to bestow particular attention upon the sanitary condition of the camps and men. The prevention of disease is the highest object of medical science.

"Very respectfully,

"Your obedient servant,

"JONA. LETTERMAN,
Medical Director."

It will be perceived that the preservation of the health of the Army was, in my opinion, a matter of paramount importance. My efforts to reduce the amount of disease to the lowest possible ratio were unceasing, and my attention was constantly given to the location and police of the camps, to the proper arrangement of the hospitals, and to the care bestowed upon the sick and wounded. I found that the labors of Dr. Webster were greater than one officer could perform, and appointed Surgeon J. H. Taylor, U. S. Vols., Medical Inspector for the Army. The services of these gentlemen were exceedingly valuable, not only as Inspectors, but as assistants on the field of battle. They were able, impartial, and fearless in the discharge of all their duties, and reflected credit on the department of which they were officers.

I am convinced that there exists in the minds of many, perhaps the majority, of line officers, a very imperfect conception of the position of Medical officers, and the objects for which a Medical Staff was instituted. It is a popular delusion that the highest duties of Medical officers are performed in prescribing a drug or amputating a limb; and the troops frequently feel the ill effect of this obsolete idea, and are often unnecessarily broken down in health and compelled to endure suffering which would have been avoided did commanders take a comprehensive view of this important subject. It is a matter of surprise that such a prejudice should exist in this enlightened age, particularly among highly intelligent men; and it were well if commanding officers would disabuse their minds of it, and permit our armies to profit more fully by the beneficial advice of those who, for years, have made the laws of life a study, and who are therefore best able to counteract the influences which so constantly tend to undermine the health of an army and destroy its efficiency. A corps of Medical officers was not established solely for the purpose of attending the wounded and sick; the proper treatment of these sufferers is certainly a matter of very great importance, and is an imperative duty, but the labors of Medical officers cover a more extended field. The leading idea, which should be constantly kept in view, is to strengthen the hands of the Commanding General by keeping his army in the most vigorous health, thus rendering it, in the highest degree, efficient for enduring fatigue and privation, and for fighting. In this view, the duties of such a corps are of vital importance to the success of an army, and commanders seldom appreciate the full effect of their proper fulfilment. Medical officers should possess a thorough knowledge of the powers, wants, and capabilities of the human system, the effect of food, raiment, and climate, with all its multiplied vicissitudes, the influences for evil which surround the health of an army, and the means necessary to combat them successfully. They should also possess quickness of perception, a sound judgment, promptness in action, and skill in the treatment of medical and surgical diseases. It is the interest of the Government, aside from all motives of humanity, to bestow the greatest possible care upon its wounded and sick, and to use every means to preserve the health of those who are well, since the greater the labor given to the preservation of health, the greater will be the number for duty, and the more attention bestowed upon the sick and wounded, the more speed-ily will they perform the duties for which they were employed, or be discharged from a service which they can no longer benefit. When Medical officers consider this subject attentively, all their high and important duties will naturally occur to them. The measures resulting from my views of the duty of a Medical Staff exerted a beneficial influence upon the troops, whose dispirited condition was so perceptible after the battle of Fredericksburg. Whatever may have been the cause of this depressed feeling, there was no doubt of its existence; and constant watchfulness and deter-mination were required of Medical officers to detect the numerous cases of feigned sickness, to prevent the lists of sick being swelled by men who magnified trifling ailments to avoid duty, and to break up the existing mania for being sent to General Hospitals, from which they too seldom returned to their commands. Deser-tion was announced, in orders from headquarters, to be " of alarming frequency ; " all Provost Marshals were " called upon to redouble their vigilance to pre-vent it." When such habits prevail, there cannot exist among the troops that feeling which should actuate them in sight of the enemy, whom they were liable at any time to meet again upon the field of battle. Many of the labors of this department were inter- rupted by the movement of the Army in the latter part of January. After the troops had returned to their camps, General Burnside was relieved, and Major-General Hooker placed in command of the Army on the 26th of that month. From that time until the latter part of April, frequent storms of snow and rain swept over the country, making the roads almost impassable, and every one exceedingly uncom- fortable. The few clear days were not sufficient to dry up the deep mud for which this part of Virginia became so famous, and which certainly will not be soon forgotten by those who were compelled to live in it during that winter. Timber was abundant during the early part of the season, but, toward its close, became very scarce and difficult to obtain, owing to the wide-spreading sea of mud and mire.

The uncertainty regarding the length of time the Army would remain inactive prevented the men from being properly protected from the inclemencies of the weather; and since the *tente d'abri*, the only shelter provided by Government, was inadequate for that purpose, the troops were left to their own ingenuity to shield themselves from the rain, the snow, and the cold. The Army was considered an active army in the field, and not in winter quarters, as it should have been, and as it was, so far as any operations against the enemy were involved. The men were left to burrow and shelter themselves as well as they were able; in some cases they occupied the log huts constructed by the enemy when he held this portion of the country at the beginning of the war; in other instances, they excavated the earth, from six to eighteen inches, and over this built a pen of logs, two or three feet high, and covered by the shelter tent or brush and dirt. Many regimental commanders took little interest in the welfare of their men; and although many of the evils inseparable from this want of attention were corrected by the Medical Department, I deemed it expedient to bring the subject to the notice of the Commanding General in the following note:

"HEADQUARTERS, ARMY OF THE POTOMAC,
Medical Director's Office, March 9, 1863.

"GENERAL: I have the honor to invite the attention of the Commanding General to a practice quite prevalent in this Army: that of excavating the earth, building a hut over the hole, and covering it over with brush and dirt or canvas. This system is exceedingly pernicious, and must have a deleterious effect upon the health of the troops occupying these

abominable habitations. They are hot-beds for low
forms of fever, and when not productive of such diseases, the health of the men is undermined, even if
they are not compelled to report sick. I strongly recommend that all troops that are using such huts be
directed at once to discontinue their use, and that they
be moved to new ground, and either build new huts
or live in tents. I also recommend that in huts covered by canvas, the covering be removed at least
twice a week, if the weather will permit, and that the
men throughout the Army be compelled to hang their
bedding in the open air every clear day: in huts not
built over an excavation, but covered with brush and
dirt or other material which cannot be removed, that
such apertures, as the Medical Directors may deem
necessary, be made in them, to allow light and ventila-
tion. I am convinced of the propriety of these suggestions from information which I have derived from
reports of inspections, made by my orders, within the
past few weeks, in order to be informed of the condition of the Army, and from my own observations.

"I am, General, very respectfully,
"Your obedient servant,
"JONA. LETTERMAN,
Medical Director.
"Brig.-Gen. S. WILLIAMS,
Adjutant-General, Army of the Potomac."

A low grade of fever, bearing in some of its features a resemblance to typhus fever, appeared in a part which had been quartered by its commander in old huts built by the enemy two years before. The regiment was at once compelled to vacate these huts and to occupy tents pitched upon new ground, and the disease speedily disappeared. I gave a great deal of attention to " police " in the widest meaning of the term, and it was very generally enforced within the camps, some of which were even decorated handsomely with evergreens.

During the latter part of January, diarrhœa, and fevers of a typhoid type, prevailed to a greater extent than was warranted by the circumstances in which the Army was placed. Symptoms of scurvy also began to appear. The ratio of cases of the first disease treated during this month, was 68.12 per thousand of the mean strength, and for those of typhus, typhoid, and typho-malarial fevers (taken together), 2.18 per thousand. Nor did the patients recover as rapidly as I thought they should, in view of the care and skill bestowed upon their treatment. The low vitality of the men was caused, in my opinion, by the want of fresh vegetables. I examined the issues, and found that, in addition to the usual abundant rations, large quantities of potatoes had been issued at the principal depot of commissary supplies. I was

not yet convinced that I had attributed this low
degree of vitality to the wrong cause; and more minute
inquiry proved that, while large supplies of potatoes
had been issued, as I have just remarked, the troops
received in some cases a very small quantity, and in
others none at all. To secure to the men the vegetables procured for them by the indefatigable Chief
Commissary, Colonel Clarke (who filled his important position so agreeably, and so well), I addressed
the following communication to the Medical Directors
of Corps, on the 3d of February:

"DOCTOR: The issue of fresh vegetables and occa-
sional changes of diet, are indispensable to the health
and consequent efficiency of the troops. The authority
of Medical officers in securing such issues is entirely
advisory; but it is the imperative duty of all Medical
officers, and especially of Medical Directors, to represent to their military commanders the necessity of
having them made regularly. Fresh potatoes should
be issued three times and onions twice a week, and
fresh bread at all times when possible. When onions
are not to be procured, a double allowance of potatoes should be issued. You will at once request the
commander of your corps to direct the commissaries
in his command to make the issues above mentioned,
and it is enjoined upon you not to relax your efforts

in this matter, so vitally important to the health of the troops, and the interests of the service. You will please direct each regimental Surgeon to state, in the "Remarks" on his weekly report of sick, how often these issues have been made during the preceding week, which you will condense in the "Remarks" on your weekly report to this office. You will please report to this office what action you have taken in pursuance of these instructions, and at the expiration of two weeks make a full report on the subject.

"Very respectfully,

"Your obedient servant,

"JONA. LETTERMAN,

Medical Director."

On the 7th of February the Commanding General, at the suggestion of Colonel Clarke, ordered that subordinate commissaries should show good reasons why they had not issued fresh and dried vegetables, and fresh bread, whenever these articles had not been furnished by them to the troops. The effect of these measures was soon apparent. The sickness began to subside, the patients to recover more rapidly, and the general health of the Army to improve. The ratio of cases of diarrhœa in February was 54.12 per thousand, and for those of the fevers before mentioned, 2.80 per thousand. In all measures for improving

the health of the troops, I was heartily assisted by
the Medical Directors of Corps, and the officers of the
department generally, each one of whom (with rare
exceptions) felt it his duty to do all in his power to
increase the efficiency of his department, and in this
way to augment the strength of the army to which
he belonged. The condition of the Army, and the
effect of the means adopted to preserve the health of
the troops, are shown in the following communication :

" HEADQUARTERS, ARMY OF THE POTOMAC,
MEDICAL DIRECTOR'S OFFICE,
Camp near Falmouth, Virginia, April 4, 1863.

" GENERAL: I have the honor to submit, for the
information of the Commanding General, the enclosed
reports on the sickness of this Army. The paper
marked ' A ' shows the whole number of sick in this
Army to be, on the 28th of March ult., ten thousand
five hundred and seventy-two. The Corps exhibiting
the greatest ratio of sick, are those in which there is
the greatest number of new regiments. Thus the
First Corps, having a ratio of 90.02 per thousand, has,
according to the data in this office, eighteen new and
twenty-one old regiments. The Sixth Corps, with a
ratio of 46.16 per thousand, has only four new and
thirty old regiments. The ratio for the whole
Army is 67.64 per thousand.

When it is considered that, since the 1st of February, less than eight hundred sick have been sent beyond the lines of this Army (excepting those of the Ninth Corps, which was ordered away), the ratio of sick is small. The paper marked 'B,' taken from the monthly sick reports of January and February, gives more explicit information regarding the health of the Army. It shows that all the more serious diseases to which troops in camp are liable, and especially those which depend upon neglect of sanitary precautions and bad diet, have decreased in a marked degree during the month of February. This paper shows that during this month typhoid fevers decreased twenty-eight per cent., and diarrhœas thirty-three per cent.; and I have every reason to expect that the reports for March (which have not yet been received) will exhibit a continued decrease. Numerous reports, made to this office, refer to the general improvement in the health, tone, and vigor of those who are not reported sick—an improvement which figures will not exhibit—but which is apparent to officers whose attention is directed to the health of the men. This favorable state of the health of the Army, and the decrease in the severity of the cases of disease is, in a great measure, to be attributed to the improvement in the diet of the men, commenced about the 1st of February, by the issue of fresh bread

and fresh vegetables, which has caused the disappear-
ance of the symptoms of scurvy, that in January
began to assume a serious aspect throughout the
Army; to the increased attention to sanitary regulations, both in camps and hospitals; to the more general practice of cooking by companies, and to the zeal
and energy displayed by the Medical Directors of
Corps, and the Medical officers of this Army generally, in inculcating the absolute necessity of cleanliness, and attention to the precautions for preserving
the health of the troops, which the united experience
of the armies of Europe and our own has shown to
be indispensable to their efficiency. I have unceas-
ingly impressed upon all officers of this department,
the primary importance of carrying into effect sanitary measures to *prevent* sickness, and my directions
and suggestions have been carried out with an intelligence and zeal which it affords me great satisfaction
to bring to the notice of the Commanding General.
It also affords me pleasure to state that the Medical
officers have found their commanders, with very few
exceptions, willing to carry into effect their suggestions to this end.

"Much, very much remains to be done; but the
earnestness and ability of the Medical officers of this
Army, to which I have alluded, and to which much
of the improvement in the health of the troops is due,

give the assurance that, so far as depends upon their exertions, nothing will be left undone to raise to a still higher degree the effective fighting strength of the Army of the Potomac.

> " I am, General, very respectfully,
> " Your obedient servant,
> " JONA. LETTERMAN,
> *Medical Director.*
>
> " Brigadier-General S. WILLIAMS,
> *Adjutant-General, Army of the Potomac.*"

For the month of March the ratio per thousand, of typhoid fevers, was 4.22, of diarrhœa 49.05. The ratio for the former disease in the month of April was 3.78, and for diarrhœa 33.96. On the 25th of that month, a few days before the battle of Chancellorsville, the ratio per thousand for the whole Army, which numbered, exclusive of cavalry, one hundred and forty thousand eight hundred and ten, was 44.58. The last of this month showed a decrease of forty-one per cent. in the ratio of typhoid fever, compared with that of January, and in diarrhœa and dysentery a decrease of more than fifty per cent.

The weather during February and March was much more inclement than in the month of January, yet the health of the Army steadily improved. The latter part of April was mild and dry, but not sufficiently so to account for the decrease in sickness. The Corps of cavalry (which on the 4th of April was over seventeen thousand strong) is not included in the calculation of the ratio for the Army, as it was absent on an expedition, endeavoring to destroy General Lee's communications with Richmond. My anticipations were realized, as will be perceived from the fact that this Army, which numbered over one hundred and forty thousand, infantry and artillery, had, in defiance of the numerous and powerful influences for evil acting upon the health of the men, a sick report under four and a half per cent. Not only was the percentage small, but those not on the lists of sick, were in vigorous health, and in the buoyant spirits arising therefrom. More soldiers die by disease than by violence, and if a Medical Staff can secure their health, its officers contribute largely to the success of a campaign.

I had a twofold object in perfecting the physical condition of the troops. First, that the Commanding General should have an army upon whose health he could rely. Second, that those who might be wounded should be in a condition to bear the shock, and the operation, the suppuration, and confinement, with every prospect of recovery.

No commander ever had an army in better health or in higher spirits, no wounded ever progressed more favorably than those from the field of Chancellors-ville.

During the winter, the Medical Department was visited by Brigadier-General Muir, Deputy Medical Inspector-General, and Medical Inspector Taylor (both of the British Army), Dr. Bellows, and other distinguished gentlemen connected with the Sanitary movement in the United States. On the 13th of April I directed the establishment of division hospitals (formed of tents) for the Second, Third, Fifth, and Sixth Corps near Potomac Creek, and as near the railroad running from Aquia Creek depot to Fredericksburg as the character of the country would permit—those for the Eleventh and Twelfth Corps near Brooks' station, on the same road; those for the First Corps on the Potomac River, near the depot at the mouth of Aquia Creek; those for the cavalry on this creek, a short distance from the depot. The hospitals of each corps preserved the division organization, independent in all its appointments. They were pitched near one another, all under the general charge of one officer, and abundantly supplied with officers, nurses, cooks, medicines, etc. Those men who were seriously ill were placed in hospital tents, and those who, from some slight ailment, were unable to march, were lodged in wall, Sibley, and shelter tents. An officer of the line was, at my request, ordered to act

8

as quartermaster and commissary for all these hospitals. I desired a guard for them, but could not obtain it, although they contained about eight thousand
men, when the Army moved to Chancellorsville.

In addition to the battle reports required, I issued
the form for another report, and, in transmitting it to
Medical Directors of Corps, alluded to other matters,
as will be perceived, in the following letter:

> "HEADQUARTERS, ARMY OF THE POTOMAC,
>   *Medical Director's Office, April* 27, 1863.

"DOCTOR: I enclose you blank forms for the purpose of obtaining a report of the number of killed,
wounded, and missing, the number of men engaged,
and the Medical officers present for duty, according to
the reports of the regimental commanders, in the next
battle in which this Army may be engaged. This
report you will please send to this office at the earliest
practicable period after an engagement. You are also
desired to send a special report, in detail, of the preparations made in the Medical Department of your
Corps previous to a battle, and of its operations
during and after a battle. Hitherto the officers of
this department have been able to give but little attention to the professional history of any engagement.
The medical and surgical history of a battle is a subject of deep interest to the profession and to human-

ity; and with the opportunities afforded by the battles which may yet take place, much valuable information may be contributed by the earnest attention of Medical officers to the advancement of medical science. It must not be forgotten that they are professional men, and, as such, that it becomes them to use every effort to promote the interests and objects of the profession to which they belong. The knowledge which the officers of this department have had, and may yet have opportunities of gathering, is of such a character and of such an extent as will, when made known, go far toward filling the hiatus which exists in that branch of the science in which we are now engaged—that of military surgery; and it is hoped that they will not permit these opportunities, now within their reach, to pass without availing themselves of the advantages which they afford. Your particular attention is invited to this subject, and you are desired to call the attention of all the Medical officers in the Corps of which you are the Medical Director to its importance, and to direct that the Surgeons-in-Chief of divisions cause the Tabular Statements to be made with the strictest accuracy, and that all cases of tetanus and secondary hemorrhage be carefully noted, and that all cases of whatever nature, which are of especial interest, be, as far as possible, reported in detail. The labor and attention necessary to collect the requisite data at the time when it is most abundant, as well as of making such reports while engaged in the active duties incident to the field, are well known; but the abilities and zeal of the Medical officers of the Army of the Potomac which have already been shown, convince me that, in addition to the weighty labors which fall upon them at such periods, they are able to accomplish this, and, if necessary, still more.

"Very respectfully,
"Your obedient servant,
"JONA. LETTERMAN,
Medical Director.
"*To the Medical Directors of Corps.*"

In addition to the supplies on hand when the Army moved for Chancellorsville, I directed a large amount of battle supplies to be sent to the depot near Fredicksburg, and had made arrangements with General Ingalls, Chief Quartermaster, by which all the wagons necessary would be given to transport them to such a point as I might deem expedient. Very few of these articles were required.

That portion of the Army which engaged the enemy at Chancellorsville reached the field on the 30th of April and 1st of May. The Medical Department was, in all respects, well appointed.

The First and Sixth Corps and one division of the [illegible] were ordered to operate in the vicinity of [Fredericksburg]. The First Corps, under Major-General Reynolds, marched to the Rappahannock, about [illegible] miles below that city. "The ambulances and [wagons] of the Medical Department moved, as by [order], with the trains of each division, and at night [parked] immediately in the rear of the troops." * Two [bridges] were thrown over this river with some difficulty, the enemy making a vigorous opposition from [the] intrenchments on the south bank. As soon as the bridges were completed, a division moved over. "Before the crossing was made, the three division hospitals were established near the Fitzhugh House, and about half a mile from the river, upon a level and good road. The ambulances and hospital wagons [were] brought and parked near the hospitals. A few ambulances from each division were advanced toward the river and placed in readiness to receive the wounded from the stretcher-bearers," † each regiment which crossed having been "followed by six men from the Ambulance Corps with stretchers." Among the important operations in this corps, was an amputation, at the hip-joint, on the person of James Kelly, a pri-

* Report of Surgeon J. Theodore Heard, U. S. Vols., Medical Director First Army Corps.

. † Report of Surgeon J. Theodore Heard, U. S. Vols.

vate of Company B, Fifty-sixth Pennsylvania Volunteers, by Surgeon Edward Shippen, U. S. Vols., on the 29th of April. The upper portion of the left thigh was struck by a conical ball, producing a comminuted fracture, and lodging in the bone. The operation was performed in the field hospital, a few minutes after the receipt of the injury, with little loss of blood. The patient progressed favorably until the 14th of June, when the Army marched to Maryland. I gave orders that he should not be removed, and he (with a few other grave cases) was placed in charge of a Surgeon, with medical and surgical supplies and food. Directions were given this officer to represent to the enemy the importance of not moving him, and that he had been left because the transportation would, in all human probability, cause his death. In violation of common humanity, he was, in a few days, removed to Richmond, where he remained until early in July. On the 16th of that month he arrived at Annapolis, Maryland, much emaciated, suffering from diarrhœa, total loss of appetite, and the wound affected with hospital gangrene. He was placed in a tent by himself, and given plenty of fresh air and a generous diet. The stump was dressed with dry oakum—the only local application used. On the 15th of September his general health was much improved, the wound having assumed a healthy appearance. He was discharged, for loss of limb, on the 7th of December, 1863. The wound had healed perfectly, entirely covering the stump, which would bear pressure without pain. His general health was excellent, and he could walk about as much as any person obliged to use crutches. Nearly a year later he was in fine health, superintending a small farm which he owned in Pennsylvania. The recovery of this man was remarkable, as the only case of successful amputation at the hip-joint (on the field) that came to my notice during the war, and, I believe, the only one in this country under such circumstances.* Happy as was the result in this instance, this operation should not be performed on the field, unless it be the only means of saving the patient's life. The chances of recovery are so few that no Surgeon can be justified in resorting to an operation so grave, except under the most profound sense of duty to a patient as a professional man. No thought of adding to his surgical reputation should have the slightest influence. The operation in this case was admirably performed, within fifteen minutes after the wound had been received (I was informed by Dr. Heard, Medical Director of the First Corps), and the patient would, in all probability, have died had any other course been pursued. This Corps was

* I am indebted to Surgeon Vanderkieft, U. S. Vols., for the details of this case from the time the patient was taken to Richmond.

ordered to Chancellorsville, and upon its arrival took a position on the extreme right of the line—in a for- est with- dense undergrowth. Those who were wounded near Fredericksburg were left in their hos- pitals, abundantly supplied with every thing neces- sary for their welfare. The First Corps did not arrive in time to participate in the battle of Chancel- lorsville, and had few wounded on that field. On the 6th of May, it returned to its former camps near Belle Plain. " All the arrangements of the Medical Department and the Ambulance Corps worked with great harmony, supplies were abundant, and I firmly believe that the wounded were cared for in the best possible manner." *

The Fifth Corps, under Major-General Meade, the Eleventh, under Major-General Howard, and the Twelfth, under Major-General Slocum, marched by way of Kelly's Ford over the Rappahannock, and Ely's Ford over the Rapidan, and reached Chancel- lorsville on the 30th of April. Some slight skirmish- ing occurred on their way to this place, so appropri- ately denominated the Wilderness. On the 1st of May the division of regulars, of the Fifth Corps, on our left, advanced on the "Old Richmond Pike" toward Fredericksburg, met the enemy about a mile from Chancellorsville, and drove him about two miles,

* Report of Surgeon Heard, Medical Director of the First Corps.

to avoid being outflanked, our troops were ordered to retire. The Twelfth Corps moved on the railroad leading to Fredericksburg, and drove the enemy back, within a short distance of the Tabernacle church, when it was ordered to retire. A new line was formed, like a crescent—with the building called Chancellorsville about the middle of the line, but well to the front. Two divisions of the Second Corps, under Major-General Couch, reached the field late on the 30th of April, or early on the 1st of May. About noon on the latter day, the Third Corps, commanded by Major-General Sickles, arrived on the field. These Corps together numbered, on the 25th of April, over seventy-five thousand effective men. On the afternoon of May 2d the Twelfth Corps again advanced on the plank road, but found the enemy in strong force, and after severe fighting it was compelled to fall back to its former position. This day was passed in manœuvring, and taking up positions, until about six o'clock in the evening, when the Eleventh Corps, on our right, was suddenly attacked with great impetuosity, by a portion of the enemy's forces under Lieutenant-General (Stonewall) Jackson, Our troops fled in haste and confusion to the rear; all efforts to rally them being vain, other troops were quickly sent to this part of the field, and succeeded in checking the progress of the enemy. After dark we attempted to regain the ground lost by the flight of this Corps, and, I understood, the design was accomplished. The engagement presented a scene of the most magnificent character. The entire field was brilliantly illuminated by the incessant flashing of many guns, and the whole region resounded with the deafening roar of artillery. During this night Lieutenant-General Jackson was accidentally wounded by some of his own men, and shortly afterwards died. In him we lost a formidable enemy, and the rebellion a powerful supporter to that cause;

> "A blast from out his bugle-horn
> Were worth ten thousand men."

Before morning our line was drawn nearer to Chancellorsville. The battle proper opened about five o'clock in the morning of May 3d, and was maintained with great obstinacy for several hours, when our troops were driven from the field. A new line was formed, about three-quarters of a mile in the rear of that occupied in the beginning of the engagement, and in a short time made formidable by intrenchments, behind which the Army remained until it recrossed the Rappahannock on the night of May 5th, and returned to the vicinity of its former encampments.

The Sixth Corps, commanded by Major-General

Sedgwick, operating in the vicinity of Fredericksburg, crossed to the south bank of the Rappahannock,
on the 29th of April, about two miles below the
city, toward which it advanced.   General Sedgwick
received information that the enemy had abandoned
Marye's Heights, in the rear of the town, but on
his approach, found them occupied by the opposing
forces.   On the 3d of May at noon he ordered them
to be stormed, which was most gallantly and successfully done, by the veteran troops, in less than an hour.
He pressed on, and late in the afternoon overtook
the enemy in strong force at Salem Church, about
three miles and a half from Fredericksburg.   At daylight on the 4th Marye's heights were reoccupied by a
portion of the enemy's troops; the remainder, apparently very strongly reënforced, vigorously attacked
General Sedgwick, and made the most strenuous
efforts to capture the entire Corps, which by skilful
management and hard fighting, reached Banks's Ford,
about eight miles above the city, and recrossed the
river on the 5th of May.

The conduct of these troops elicited not only the
admiration of friends, but the encomiums of their
enemies.   Their long devotion to their gallant leader
was as conspicuous as their faithful service.   The
fatal summons that found him at his post upon the
battle-field filled many hearts with sorrow, and his

example strengthened the sacred cause to which his life was devoted, and for which he died.

From this slight sketch of the military operations it will be perceived that the Army of the Potomac was divided into unequal portions—the one moving to Chancellorsville to take the enemy on his left flank, and if possible by surprise—the other moving by Fredericksburg to join the main body in the Wilderness. Assistant-Medical Director Clements, with Medical Inspector Taylor, remained in charge of the Medical Department, near Fredericksburg; and I, with Medical Inspector Webster, accompanied General Hooker to Chancellorsville. I was informed that an order had been issued forbidding any wagons following the troops across the river, and that only two ambulances would be allowed to each division. I therefore directed all the ambulances and medicine and hospital wagons to be taken to the United States Mine ford, about six miles from Chancellorsville, and parked on the north bank of the river. Authority was given to take a very few ambulances to the front, by which we were enabled to remove the wounded of May 1st. After urgent representations I obtained permission to order a few medicine wagons to the field; not enough, however, to supply the wants of the wounded, and the defect was remedied by transporting the supplies, in the ambulances, and on horses

plies. In this way medical and surgical supplies in ample quantities were conveyed to the field
hospitals. As Fredericksburg was about ten miles
from Chancellorsville, it was my intention to remove
the wounded to that city, and thus avoid a transportation of twenty-five miles, over bad roads, to the
hospitals near Potomac Creek. The falling back of
our forces, on the 1st of May, did not present a very
encouraging prospect of moving the wounded over a
long and good road. On that evening, I determined
not to keep the wounded, but to send them, as
speedily as possible, to the hospitals prepared for
them, and subsequent events clearly demonstrated the
propriety of this course. A portion of the house
called Chancellorsville was used as an hospital for
some of the wounded of May 1st, the other portion
being occupied by the Commanding General as his
headquarters. On the afternoon of May 2d this
building came within range of the enemy's guns,
planted on his left, centre, and right, being the centre of a converging fire—a location for which Commanding Generals of the Army of the Potomac
seemed to have a peculiar partiality. Previous to
this time I had all the wounded, who could be
removed, taken further to the rear, and directed that
no more should be received in the house, as it was
evident, from the position of our line, that when the

battle opened in earnest, the building would also
come within range of his musketry. On the 2d of
May Surgeon Dougherty, Medical Director of the
Second Corps, formed his hospitals about a mile in
rear of the line of battle, in a dense forest, and by a
small stream, which gave an abundant supply of
water. As the wagons containing the hospital tents
were not allowed to come on the field, shelter was
made of boughs of the pine and other trees, and roads
were cut through the heavy undergrowth. The preparations required by the Circular for field hospitals
were made, and the stretcher-bearers sent to the front,
in rear of their regiments. On this day, few
wounded were brought in, but on the 3d the hospitals were rapidly filled by the assiduous labor of
the Ambulance Corps. The operating staff were
actively employed, the necessary operations quickly
and dexterously performed, and every thing worked
harmoniously, until our troops were driven back.
This untoward event suddenly brought these hospitals within range of the enemy's guns, from which some
shells were thrown among the wounded, killing one
and wounding five. The hospitals were speedily
removed half a mile further to the rear, and as we
held the ground selected after the repulse of the
morning, the wounded were safe from further injury.
The Medical officers of this Corps conducted them-

selves gallantly under fire—the surgical details remaining at their posts until every wounded man was removed, and orders were given them to retire. Although very few ambulances were allowed with the troops, the officers and men of the corps performed their duty so well, that no wounded within our lines were left on the field. After the requisite operations, they were sent to the hospitals near Potomac Creek, as rapidly as the limited number of ambulances would permit. The medical and surgical appliances and food were ample; after the wants of the wounded had been fully supplied, the remainder was carefully transported to the rear, so that nothing was abandoned. The conduct of Dr. Dougherty upon that field, where he freely exposed himself, for the sake of his wounded, regardless of danger, was in the highest degree commendable, and in keeping with the many sterling qualities of this excellent Surgeon.

Before the Third Corps left its camps, the Medical Director, Surgeon Thomas Sim, U. S. Volunteers, saw that " requisitions had been made for every needful supply. The convalescents, or those unable to march, as well as the sick, had been comfortably provided for in our corps hospitals at Potomac Creek. The details had been made for the division operating staff, and each Medical officer had received definite

instructions as to his particular duties on the field; in
short, every thing was ready, so far as the Medical
staff was concerned, for the coming conflict." "With
the order to march, came the notification that no ambulances or hospital wagons would be allowed to
accompany the troops"* The pack-mules and pan-
niers belonging to the Medical Department of this
Corps were therefore used in transporting supplies.
On the field the hospitals of two divisions were located at a house owned by a Mr. Chandler, about a
mile in the rear of the line of battle—where all the
needful preparations were made. The hospital of
the First Division was placed near the plank road,
about one mile west of Chancellorsville, in the rear
of its division. The Eleventh Corps, in its retreat on
the evening of the 2d ran over this hospital; this
made it no longer tenable; and the increasing prox-
imity of the enemy caused the removal of the few
wounded it contained to the hospitals of the other
divisions. The retreat of the Eleventh Corps rendered even these unsafe; the enemy threw shells into
them, and by my advice the wounded were removed
during the night of May 2d to the vicinity of the
hospitals of the Second Corps, and placed in hospitals
constructed of boughs. The repulse of our troops on

---

* Report of Surgeon Thomas Sim, U. S. Volunteers.

THE ARMY OF THE POTOMAC.   129

the 3d of May brought these hospitals within reach
of the enemy's shells, by which three men were
killed; the hospitals were again removed about two
miles to the rear, near a saw-mill, and to a large
brick house near the river. Great difficulty was experienced in removing the wounded, for want of ambulances (plenty of which were parked on the north
bank of the river); but with very great exertions on
the part of Dr. Sim and his staff, they were in a short
time out of danger, and every thing at the hospitals
speedily and " admirably arranged; the wounded were
all attended to, and well fed. That portion of the
field under our control was searched and all the
wounded brought in, and every wounded man was
safely removed across the river before the Army
commenced its march for camp.   I have seen no
battle in which the wounded were so well cared for;
and had not military necessity deprived us of the use
of our ambulance train on the south side of the river,
nearly every wounded man could have been comfortably placed in our corps hospitals (near Potomac
Creek) within twenty-four hours after the receipt of
his wounds. Of the medical officers detailed to accompany their regiments into the field, three were wounded, two of them severely; and it gives me pleasure
to testify to the bravery, faithfulness, and humanity,
displayed by the majority of the Medical officers dur-

9

ing the late battles." * Supplies in this corps were abundant. The ability, and careful regard for the wounded, displayed by Dr. Sim, place him high in the ranks of military Surgeons, but can be properly appreciated only by those who participated in his labors and difficulties.

In the engagement of a portion of the Fifth Corps on the 1st of May, the wounded (who were not numerous) were taken to some houses near the scene of action, where "they were promptly attended to, and when the order was given to fall back, were all carried to comfortable rooms at the Chancellor House, where such operations as remained to be done, were completed. Supplies of medicines, dressings, and food were abundant, and every thing made as comfortable for our poor fellows, as was possible in the field. In the morning of May 2d, as it appeared evident that the house would be under fire, in accordance with instructions from Surgeon Letterman, all the wounded, except such severe cases as were likely to be injured by the ambulance carriage, were sent to the corps hospitals in the vicinity of Potomac Creek bridge; some five or six cases only were left, and two or three of these were in a dying condition from terrible shell wounds. Assistant-Surgeon Bacon, U. S. A., and Surgeon Doolittle, Fifth

* Report of Surgeon Sim, U. S. Volunteers.

New York, were sent in charge of the train, the latter with directions to go in advance to a house on the north bank of the Rappahannock, where soup, tea, etc., were to be prepared for all in the train, the materials and the party to have them prepared having been sent to this point on the preceding day. I may add here, that this was done in the same manner for all the wounded of this corps sent to the rear subsequently."*

On the morning of May 3d, this Corps being posted near the Chancellor House, extending along the road leading to Ely's Ford, the hospitals of the Second and Third Divisions were located near the road leading to the United States Mine Ford, about one mile and a half in the rear of their divisions; that of the First Division was placed so far to the left, that it was found with some difficulty. These hospitals were furnished with every thing required for the wounded, except their tents; and great devotion was shown by the Medical officers of the Second and Third Divisions who "performed their duty nobly" and exhibited great "industry and attention to the wounded." † As the ambulances could not cross the river, the ambulance men joined their re-

* Report of Surgeon Moore, U. S. A., Medical Director of the Fifth Corps.

† Report of Surgeon John Moore, U. S. A.

spective commands, and performed their duty so well, that "scarcely an hour elapsed in any case, in this corps, from the time any man was wounded until he was carried by the stretcher-men to the field hospitals, except twelve or fourteen men, in Humphreys' Division, who fell in the advance, upon a part of the field not afterwards held by our troops." * On the 5th of May all the remaining wounded were sent to their corps hospitals, together with the supplies which had not been required. "But as there were some of the rebel wounded in each of my three hospitals, and as it was known that some of our wounded were still on the field, a Surgeon, with a liberal amount of medicines, dressings, and food was left in charge of each hospital, in accordance with instructions from the Medical Director." † It is a very great pleasure to refer to Doctor Moore's discharge of duty, and his conscientious regard for the wounded; they were appreciated by Surgeon-General Hammond, who transferred him, shortly after this battle, to a more responsible position. On the 2d of May, the hospitals of the Eleventh Corps were formed in rear of their respective divisions. Such houses as were at all suitable were put in condition to receive the wounded, and "the Surgeons were detailed, and

* Report of Surgeon John Moore, U. S. A.
† Report of Surgeon John Moore, U. S. A.

their posts, a proper detail of attendants made,
and every thing arranged in conformity with the instructions of October 30, 1862." * The retreat of
the Corps compelled the hasty evacuation of the hospitals; all the wounded who could walk were at once
sent to the rear, whither the more severely wounded
were carried in ambulances. The attack of Lieutenant-General Jackson almost completely disorganized
this Corps, and small parties of slightly wounded
men were "scattered all through the woods," who
were collected and sent to their hospitals, finally
established on the north bank of the river, from
which they were transported to their hospitals at
Brooks' Station. A number of hospital knapsacks and
cases of instruments were lost, but I was surprised
to find that the Medical Department had not suffered
more in the panic. A number of Medical officers
were taken prisoners, among whom was Surgeon
George Suckley, U. S. Volunteers, the Medical Director of the Corps, who had his clothes torn by a
bullet, and who narrowly escaped with his life. The
loss of this officer's valuable services was severely felt,
but was in part compensated by the attention he
bestowed upon our wounded who fell into the hands
of the enemy. The check experienced by the Twelfth
Corps on May 2d did not result in a large number of

* Report of Acting Medical Director Thom, U. S. Volunteers.

wounded, and these were at once carefully attended by Surgeon John McNulty, U. S. Volunteers. The position of this Corps being frequently changed before it took its final place in the line of battle, required the hospitals also to be changed. Under the most favorable circumstances, this is a laborious and vexatious task; in the Wilderness, the absence of eligible situations for hospitals, greatly increased the difficulty. Notwithstanding, the wounded of the three days' fighting were speedily removed from the field, and well attended. One of the hospitals (as in the case of the Third Corps) was run over by the Eleventh Corps, and ruined. Doctor McNulty devoted himself assiduously and successfully to the wounded of his corps; many of whom have cause gratefully to remember him.

When the Sixth Corps entered Fredericksburg on the 3d of May, and an engagement was imminent, the "hospitals were at once established in the town, put in the best state of preparation for the wounded; supplies in abundance were on hand. The charge (on Marye's Heights) was ordered at half past twelve, and the heights were taken at one o'clock P. M., and at two o'clock all the wounded, over one thousand, were within the hospitals. The hospital organization, prescribed in circular of October 30, 1862, was adhered to strictly; the care of the wounded, the despatch with which they had been attended to, and the comfort consequent thereon, met the approval of all." *   I know of no instance in which such a number of wounded were so speedily removed from the field, and so promptly and well attended as in the admirably conducted hospitals of this Corps. The wounded in the fight at Salem Church, were removed to the hospitals in the town, excepting a few taken prisoners by the enemy, who came into possession of the field as our troops moved on.   The reoccupation of Marye's Heights by the enemy gave him control of the country between the hospitals and the Corps, and also of the town.   This necessitated the removal of the wounded to the opposite side of the river.   "To remove the wounded to the north side of the river, and reëstablish communication with the Corps, now demanded the most pressing attention and diligence; the former was effected with very little difficulty; by ten o'clock our hospitals were established in tents, and all the wounded accommodated by eleven A. M.   The ambulances were then despatched to Banks' Ford; but as the pontoon bridge, on their arrival there, was found to be under the fire of the enemy, they could not proceed.   The extent of ground the Corps passed over, the enemy getting be-

* Report of Surgeon O'Leary, U. S. Volunteers, Medical Director of the Sixth Corps.

tween the hospitals and the battle-field, and being in possession of the ground upon which we fought from four P.M. on Sunday until we recrossed on Tuesday, presented obstacles to the removal of the wounded rarely experienced. Notwithstanding these embarrassments, the number of wounded left on the field, and afterwards received under flag of truce, was very small in proportion to the whole loss—only seventy-five. The system and good order which governed our hospitals, and the care our wounded received, seem now so much things of course, that I feel it unnecessary to draw attention to them. For all necessities during and immediately subsequent to the battles, our supplies on hand were abundant, and the Medical Purveyor at Falmouth afforded all articles subsequently required." * "The good management of the hospitals and their excellent organization" is attributed by Surgeon O'Leary "to the zeal, energy, and experience of the Surgeons-in-Chief of Division," Surgeons Taylor, Allen, and Holman. Too much credit can scarcely be given them for the manner in which the order for field hospitals was carried out; their hospitals were not surpassed by any that I have ever seen upon the field of battle. I cannot refrain from saying, that the manner in which the Medical De-

---

* Report of Surgeon O'Leary, U. S. V.

partment of this whole Corps was conducted by Surgeon O'Leary, gave evidence that this valuable officer combined great professional and executive ability, with an earnestness and devotion to duty rarely equalled.

The headquarters of General Hooker were much exposed to the fire of the enemy. On the 3d of May a round shot struck the stone steps of the portico, upon which the Commanding General stood, watching the progress of the battle, knocked down a solid wooden pillar, which struck him, and felled him to the floor. Being within a few feet of him at the time of the accident, I saw him fall, and was instantly with him, and had him taken to his room; he was very much stunned by the blow, although no bones were broken. The rumor spread rapidly that General Hooker was killed, and to dispel that idea, he appeared to the troops, though scarcely able to sit upon his horse. The effect of this blow and fall, lasted for some hours. On the night of May 4th it was decided to recross the river the following night. On the morning of the 5th I received an order from Major-General Butterfield, Chief of Staff, to remove all the wounded without delay, but to use only those ambulances on the south side of the river. The Provost Marshal at the river had orders to allow no ambulances to return when they had once passed to the north bank. The propriety of removing the wounded as rapidly as possible on the 1st of May was now very apparent; their removal at this time, with the few ambulances allowed on the field would have been an impossibility. As it was, the order was impracticable; and after much solicitation I was permitted, late in the day, to manage the matter in my own way. I then ordered a sufficient number of ambulances from the north side of the river, and all the wounded were taken across before the troops began to pass the stream.

On the 3d of May nearly twelve hundred of our wounded fell into the hands of the enemy. As soon as the Army returned to the position occupied before the march to Chancellorsville, my earnest attention was devoted to the alleviation of their sufferings, and their speedy removal to their own hospitals. The latter being a subject of negotiation between the Commanders of the respective forces, I had no power to act, but simply to give my advice when called upon for it. On the 8th of May twenty-six Medical officers, and five army wagons, laden with blankets, stimulants, lint, bandages, chloroform, beef stock, etc., under charge of Dr. Asch, U. S. A., were despatched for the relief of these men. On the same day the Commanding General, at my request, directed six hundred rations of fresh bread, beef, coffee, sugar, salt and candles, to be sent to Banks' Ford, for our wounded in that vicinity, and on the following day, sent to Chancellorsville two thousand rations of the same articles. There was no bridge at the United States Mine Ford, and the officers and supplies were much delayed in reaching the wounded. It was necessary to convey them over the river on a raft, and to use the rebel transportation to carry them to their destination. The articles sent " were invaluable, and an immediate change for the better could be perceived among the patients" * upon their arrival. They reached the sufferers " very opportunely; the wounded were cheered by the knowledge that some provision was being made for them, and many lives were saved by the free use of stimulants, and the nourishing food distributed." † It was very gratifying to learn, some time afterwards, that the wounded freely expressed their conviction (before any assistance was sent) that the Medical Director was doing all in his power to relieve them, and have them brought to their own hospitals. Nineteen Medical officers (including Medical Inspector Webster, who voluntarily remained) were taken prisoners; these, with the twenty-six sent after the battle, were reported by Surgeon Suckley to be more than were

* Report of Surgeon Lyster, Fifth Michigan Volunteers.
† Report of Dr. Asch, U. S. A.

required. General Lee offered free passage to our ambulance trains to Chancellorsville and other points, for the purpose of avoiding the suffering that would be endured if our wounded were carried in the enemy's transportation, and transferred to our ambulances. When this information was received, on the 11th of May, I advised a pontoon bridge to be thrown over the Rappahannock, at the United States Mine Ford, that our trains, capable of carrying all the wounded at one trip, might at once pass over, *en route* to Chancellorsville, and return without delay. This suggestion (unfortunately, I think, for these men) was not regarded, and an attempt was made to ferry them over on a raft constructed of " two pontoon boats supporting a platform large enough to take on two ambulances or twelve stretcher-men." *   I again urged upon the Chief of Staff the necessity for the bridge ; the river was not fordable for ambulances, on account of the depth of water, the rocky bed of the stream, and the remains of a canal on the south bank. Instead of the bridge being laid, some men were sent to dig down the banks of the canal. Several communications had passed between the commanders of the two armies, regarding the transfer of our wounded, and as the prospect of their speedy arrival was not encouraging, I suggested to the Commanding

* Report of Surgeon Irvin, Third New York, Excelsior Brigade.

General that the matter be left in the hands of the
Medical Directors of the respective armies, to which
he acceded, and sent General Lee a note, making that
proposition. That commander consented to it, and
had an interview with his Medical Director, Surgeon Guild, under a flag of truce. It was, I presume,
in consequence of this interview, that General Lee
wrote to the Commanding General, offering free passage to our trains. On the 11th of May I sent four
hundred and fifty ambulances, carrying two thousand
seven hundred pounds of beef stock, to the United
States Mine Ford, to be in readiness to cross at the
earliest moment. I also sent ambulances to Banks'
Ford and Fredericksburg. Reports from some of our
Medical officers in the enemy's lines induced me to
believe that, if the delay in removing our wounded
continued, the enemy would refuse to give them to us.
Once more I urged upon the Chief of Staff the *great
necessity* which existed, in my opinion, for having
our wounded brought within our lines at once, and
strongly advised the bridge to be laid. This officer telegraphed to the Commanding General (who
had gone to Washington) for his decision, and the
measure I had so earnestly solicited was ordered immediately. The bridge was laid, late on the 13th
of May, on which day I had increased the number of
ambulances to five hundred and fifty. On the 14th,

these were taken over the river; they proceeded to
the different localities where the wounded had been
collected by Surgeon Suckley and Assistant-Surgeon
Webster, and at half past nine o'clock on the evening
of the 15th these sufferers, numbering eleven hundred
and sixty, were within our lines. On the 13th I sent
Medical Inspector Taylor to the place of crossing, to
superintend their transportation from that point to
their hospitals.

The trains of each Corps were halted as they
crossed to the north bank of the river, refreshment
given the men, and such professional care bestowed
by the Medical officers accompanying them as the
cases required. Only a small number were brought
from Banks' Ford and from Fredericksburg.

I have alluded to the large hospitals formed of
tents near Potomac Creek, to which the wounded
were sent. The Medical officers would have been
spared a vast amount of labor had these hospitals not
been established; but the advantages of this system
to patients and Surgeons were very important. The
men were kept under the care of their own Medical
officers, with whom they had passed through many
battles, and in whom they had every confidence.
These officers had heretofore been unable to see the
issue of their professional labors upon the field. In
the numerous engagements through which many of

them had passed, they had become very skilful opera-
tors, and I desired to give them the experience derived
only from treatment *after* the operation. The knowledge thus gained would be of great benefit to the
wounded from another battle. I believe it is the correct principle, when the exigencies of the service will
permit, that the sick and wounded should be kept
with the army—treated by their own Surgeons. The
history of this war has proved that life in a General
Hospital tends to destroy the good qualities of a sol-
dier, and nowhere are these so well preserved as with
their comrades in the camp.

On the 3d of May I had directed the hospital
tents in the depot at Aquia Creek to be distributed
to the different hospitals, pitched and made ready for
the wounded; and within twenty-four hours Assistant-Medical Director Clements had executed the
order. About two thousand wounded had been sent
to Washington, but, with few exceptions, the seriously
injured were placed in these hospitals, which were
under the direction of the Medical Directors of the
Corps to which they belonged. Many of the gravest
cases had lain for days in the hands of the enemy,
where it was impossible they could receive the care
and treatment their injuries demanded. The great
majority soon exhibited the beneficial effects of
proper treatment—good diet, shelter, abundance of

light, and pure air. The Medical Directors of Corps
and the Surgeons in immediate charge devoted all
their energy and skill to the welfare of these men;
the hospitals were kept in order; attention to duty
was strictly enjoined upon every one, and cheerfully
given; good surgery prevailed, and many cases which
seemed hopeless when brought from the field, where
they had lain prisoners so long, became better, and
finally recovered. I have never seen better hospitals.
This opinion was entertained by the professional and
unprofessional men who visited them, and I regretted
the necessity which compelled me to break them up
about the middle of June in consequence of the march
of the Army into Maryland and Pennsylvania.

With a Medical Staff like that of the Army of
the Potomac, such hospitals will always be successful.
Nine thousand five hundred and eighteen men were
wounded in this battle—six hundred and twenty-four
officers and eight thousand eight hundred and ninety-
four enlisted men. While engaged in the harassing
efforts to obtain our wounded from Chancellorsville,
and in discharging the various duties incident to the
largest field hospitals which, I believe, ever existed,
the warm weather of spring and early summer was
upon us, and my attention was once more devoted to
the inauguration of such measures as would most
surely preserve the Army from disease. Before the

troops had recrossed the Rappahannock, the Commanding General, upon my recommendation, ordered
that no troops should occupy ground upon which
camps had been formed during the winter, and on the
11th I sent him a note on the subject. On the next
day I addressed him the following letter upon the
means I considered proper for preserving the health
of the men:

"HEADQUARTERS, ARMY OF THE POTOMAC,
May 12, 1863.

"GENERAL: Respectfully referring to my letter of
the 11th instant, in which I invited the attention of
the Commanding General to the necessity which I
conceived to exist for prohibiting the occupation by
the troops of the same ground upon which the men
encamped during the past winter, I have the honor to
submit the following suggestions, which, if carried
into effect, will, I believe, be of the greatest value in
maintaining the health and efficiency of the Army.

"In the selection of camping grounds, that should
be selected which has natural drainage, and all low-
lying and bottom-lands, and lands in the vicinity of
stagnant water, should be avoided. Every camp
should be thoroughly ditched by main ditches,
eighteen inches deep, and the ground around the
tents drained by ditches leading into the main ditches
of the camp.

10

" Camps should, whenever possible, be pitched in the vicinity of running streams or of living springs, and the use of surface water, or that from holes dug two or three feet in the ground, should, by all means, be avoided. Camps should not be formed in the woods, but upon the open ground, where a full and free exposure to the sun and air can be obtained, and the tents should be pitched *upon* the ground, and in no case should the men be permitted to excavate the earth underneath them, nor should the distance between the tents be less than that required by the Regulations. The tents should be struck twice a week, and the ground over which they have been pitched be exposed to the direct rays of the sun and to the winds, and, if possible, they should be placed upon new ground, if only a few feet distant, once a week. The troops should be required to procure the small boughs from the pine-tree and spread them thickly upon the ground covered by the tents, and should renew them once a week; these will keep them from sleeping on the ground, which they should not be permitted to do. The cooking, especially when in camp, should be done by companies, and not by individuals or by squads, and for this purpose two men should be detailed from each company as cooks, one relieved every month, thus allowing each one detailed to be on this duty for two months.

"The importance of police, general and special, cannot be too highly regarded. The blankets and bedding of the men should be removed from the tents and exposed to the sun and air daily, when the weather will permit. Every tent, and the ground in and about and between the camps, should be thoroughly policed daily, and all refuse matter, or filth of whatever kind, be buried at least three feet under ground, and all dead animals, and all offal and blood from slaughtered animals, should be at once buried at least four feet beneath the surface, and the refuse matters from stables and wagon-yards should be buried two feet under ground, or burned.

"In every camp sinks should be dug and *used*, and the men on no consideration be allowed to commit any nuisance anywhere within the limits of this Army. The sinks should be eight feet deep, if the ground will permit, and have earth, to the depth of six inches, thrown in every evening, and, when filled to within three feet of the surface, be entirely filled up with earth, and new ones dug. No one thing produces a more deleterious effect upon the health than the emanations from the human body, especially when in process of decay; and this one item of police should receive especial attention. Holes should be dug near each company kitchen, in which should be cast all the refuse matters from it, and, when filled to within two feet of the surface, should be filled with earth and new ones dug.

"The men should be required to wear their hair cut short, bathe twice a week, and put on clean underclothing at least once a week. The troops should have their breakfast as soon as they rise.

"Spasmodic efforts, in a matter of such paramount importance as police in an army, can be of no service, and I recommend that regimental and other commanders be required to see that these suggestions, if they meet the approval of the Commanding General, be fully and continuously carried into effect.

"I am, General, very respectfully,
"Your obedient servant,
"JONA. LETTERMAN,
Medical Director.

"Brig.-Gen. S. WILLIAMS,
"*Assistant Adjutant-General,*
Army of the Potomac."

With the exception of the first paragraph, the Commanding General published this letter in general orders, and directed the suggestions contained in it to be "strictly observed by all concerned," and made it "the duty of corps and other independent commanders, as well as of officers of the Inspector-General's Department, to enforce a compliance with the same." In a very short time the camps were in excellent order. They were laid out regularly, with wide and well-graded streets between the companies, descending to a deep ditch on either side, into which entered the smaller ditches between the tents. These (generally the *tentes d'abri*) were raised about two feet from the ground, protected from the sun by bowers neatly constructed of pine and cedar boughs, and in them beds were made of poles, covered with small branches of the same trees. Everywhere great cleanliness prevailed, and the great majority of the camps were decorated with arches of evergreen, containing the designation of the companies and regiments, and various devices. At this time I began to make a minute personal inspection of the entire Army, and had inspected the First and Sixth Corps, when the order to march for Maryland was received. While these matters were in progress, I gave directions for the collection and preservation of specimens of gunshot injuries for the Army Medical Museum at Washington. In the early part of June it was discovered that the enemy had sent at least a portion of his forces to the ill-starred Valley of the Shenandoah. A reconnoissance was made by the cavalry and a body of infantry, when it was ascertained that the entire army of the enemy was moving toward Maryland.

At this time Colonel B. F. Davis fell, fighting at

the head of his regiment, in the cavalry engagement at Beverly Ford. This officer, who so successfully extricated his regiment from Harper's Ferry when that post was surrendered by General Miles—who fought so gallantly on our march through Virginia in the autumn of 1862—had been my companion in more than one campaign among the Indians; my mess-mate at stations far beyond the haunts of civil-ized men. This long, familiar intercouse produced the warmest admiration for his noble character, which made him sacrifice friends and relatives to uphold the flag under which he was born, and defend the Con-stitution of his country. His young and gallant Ad-jutant nobly avenged his death upon the spot.

Our Army was ordered to follow the hostile forces. On the morning of the 12th of June I there-fore began removing the wounded, in which I was sustained by the Commanding General, who, on the evening of that day, desired they might be removed with despatch. The railroad from Fredericksburg to Aquia Creek depot had a single track, with short "sidings." Over this road had to be transported, in a very short time, over nine thousand wounded and sick, with all the hospital tents, medical and surgical supplies, stores, etc., etc., required for their care, to-gether with the accumulated supplies of the Quarter-master's, Commissary, and Ordnance Departments, with the supplies, baggage, and stores of various kinds always collected by an army in camp. I sent Medical Inspector Taylor to Aquia Creek to receive the wounded and send them to Washington. The entire Army had left on the 14th of June, on which day the headquarters were moved to Dumfries, Virginia, and, before six o'clock in the evening, all the wounded and sick, numbering nine thousand and twenty-five, had left the depot at Aquia for Washington. With the exception of a few iron bedsteads, destroyed by orders of one of the Corps commanders (unnecessarily, I think), all the hospital tents and supplies of every kind were sent to Alexandria, Virginia.

The network of telegraph wires, made by the Signal Corps, enabled me to regulate the shipment of this large number of men without difficulty or accident. I had directed that all who could not sit up, or who would be injured by so doing, should be carried by hand upon the beds they occupied in the hospitals (some of which were more than a mile from the railway), the beds placed upon hay in the cars, removed carefully from the train and placed in the transports, so that these sufferers should not be removed from the beds on which they lay in the camp hospitals until they reached the hospitals in Washington. Medical officers, with supplies, accompanied every train, and, when required, were sent with their men to Washington. Many of these, cases of amputations and fractures, were so comfortably transported that they were heard singing while on their way. My orders " to Medical Directors of Corps, in regard to the manner in which the wounded should be shipped, were carefully observed in every instance. Every such patient was transported on the cot he had occupied in the hospital, so that it was impossible he should suffer any detriment during the passage, or even whilst being transferred from the cars to the transports. Many of those most severely wounded, cases in which the femur was extensively fractured, assured me they had not suffered the slightest discomfort or fatigue up to the time of their being placed on the transports. Their subsequent transportation, I have been informed, was equally successful." *

The Army continued moving northward, with its cavalry well out upon the left, fighting daily with the cavalry of the enemy for the passes in the range of mountains separating the two armies, which were marching in almost parallel lines to Maryland, the enemy somewhat in advance when he crossed the Potomac on the 26th of June. I have heretofore given the allowance of transportation I arranged for the Medical Department in the autumn of 1862. On the 19th of June this allowance was reduced by order

* Report of Medical Inspector Taylor.

of the Commanding General, notwithstanding my verbal and written opinion against such reduction, which compelled this department to send away a large portion of its hospital tents, mess-chests, and other articles necessary upon the battle-field, and proved, as I foresaw it would, a source of embarrassment and suffering, which might have been avoided. The Army was then on its way to Maryland, in the expectation of a battle, but where the battle would be fought no one could reasonably conjecture. To guard against a deficiency in medical and surgical supplies, I directed Assistant-Surgeon Brinton, U. S. A., on the 25th of June (Headquarters being at Fairfax Court House, Virginia), to go to Washington, obtain the supplies I had previously ordered to be packed, and proceed with them to Frederick, Maryland. On the 28th of June Dr. Brinton reached that city with twenty-five army wagon loads of battle supplies, and, as the Army advanced, he proceeded to Taneytown, Maryland, beyond which place he was not permitted, by the Commanding General, to go until after the battle of Gettysburg.

Major-General Meade assumed command of the Army on the 28th of June, at Frederick, Maryland. On the 30th we reached Taneytown, Maryland, a village thirteen or fourteen miles from Gettysburg, Pennsylvania. On the 1st of July a reconnoissance

in force was made in the vicinity of Gettysburg by
Major-General Reynolds, in command of the First
and Eleventh Corps, and a small body of cavalry. A
severe engagement ensued, in which General Reynolds
was killed, and our troops were driven back to the
crest of the hill, south of the town, all our wounded
falling into the hands of the enemy. Our movements
having depended, to a certain extent, upon those of
the enemy, were not determined until the evening of
July 1st, when the result of the reconnoissance of
General Reynolds was known. The Army was at
once put in motion; the Commanding General left for
Gettysburg near midnight. The battle (proper)
began on the 2d, and ended on the 3d of July. It is
not necessary to give the details of this momentous
engagement, upon which, for two days, the fate of our
country hung wavering in the balance. The result of
it is well known. But only an eye-witness can do
justice to the bravery of the troops on both sides, the
obstinacy with which they fought—the enemy determined to conquer; our Army determined to defeat
him. It was a field of blood, on which the demon of
Destruction revelled.

Our line was like a horse-shoe, and many of the
shells from the long-ranged guns of the enemy passed
entirely over the ground enclosed by our troops. On
the 1st of July, before the result of the reconnois-

[...] of General Reynolds was known, the Command-
[...] General ordered that "Corps Commanders and
[...] Commander of the Artillery Reserve will at once
[...] the rear all their trains (excepting ammuni-
[...] wagons and the ambulances), parking these be-
[...] Union Mills and Westminster." On the 2d,
[...] the battle was in progress, the trains (including
[...] hospital wagons and the train of battle supplies,
[...] charge of Dr. Brinton) were sent still further
[...] rear, about twenty-five miles distant from the
[...] field. In most of the Corps the medicine
wagons (of which, as I have remarked, a sufficient
number could never be procured) were taken to the
front with the ambulances, and furnished supplies for
[...] immediate wants. The exposure of the whole
field, occupied by our troops, to the fire of the enemy
(we were driven from the cabin selected as Headquarters both on the 2d and 3d), made it impossible
to place the hospitals in rear of their divisions. Most
of them were placed entirely out of the enclosure
formed by the line of battle. Even the temporary
halting-places, in the rear of the columns, were so
unsafe, that we were obliged to abandon them. It is
not necessary to enter into the details of the location
and management of the hospitals, as it would be little
else than repetition of what I have said of them
before. The want of tents, cooking apparatus, etc.,

occasioned by the recent orders, was to me, in common
with all the Medical officers, a cause of the deepest
regret, and to the wounded of much unnecessary suffering.   Without proper means the Medical Department can no more take care of the wounded than the
army can fight a battle without ammunition.   The
Medical Department *had* these means, but military
necessity deprived it of a portion of them, and would
not permit the remainder to come upon the field.   As
soon as the battle terminated, I requested the Commanding General to allow me to order to the hospitals
the wagons containing the tents, etc., and the extra
supplies. After much persuasion, he gave me authority
to order half the number of wagons.   I at once gave
directions to send for them, and also for the remainder
as soon as I could obtain permission to do so.   These
were of much service when they arrived, but they
could not reach the field in time to protect the wounded from the drenching rain which fell after the battle.
The twenty-five army wagons, under charge of Dr.
Brinton, reached the field the day after the battle.
On the 5th and 6th I ordered additional supplies from
Baltimore and Philadelphia to be sent to Gettysburg
so that they would reach that place before those
brought by Dr. Brinton were exhausted.

Houses and barns, but chiefly the woods, were
used as hospitals, and the wounded, necessarily, en-

dured much suffering. Had the weather been pleasant, much of this' suffering would not have occurred.
In the Twelfth Corps the order reducing the Medical
transportation had not been carried out; nor was the
order to send all the wagons to the rear observed, so
that its Medical Department had the full allowance
of supplies upon the field, in consequence of which
the Medical Director of that Corps wrote: "It is
with extreme satisfaction that I can assure you that
it enabled me to remove the wounded from the field,
shelter, feed them, and dress their wounds, within six
hours after the battle ended, and to have every capital operation performed within twenty-four hours
after the wound was received." *   I have every reason
to believe the same excellent results would have been
experienced in the other corps, had not my measures
been frustrated by authority from which there was
no appeal. The wounded did not lack surgical supplies, but they *did* lack accessories almost as important. Even should an army be defeated, it is better
to have the supplies for the proper care and comfort
of the wounded upon the field, and run the risk of
their capture, than that the wounded should suffer for
want of them. Lost supplies can be replenished, but
lives lost are gone forever.

* Report of Surgeon McNulty, Medical Director of the Twelfth Corps.

The Ambulance Corps performed its duty well.
Before daylight on the morning of the 4th all the
wounded within our lines (numbering on these two
days about twelve thousand) were removed to the
hospitals.   Lieutenant H. R. Clark, Fifth New York
Volunteers, and two privates were killed, seventeen
privates wounded ; seven horses were killed and five
wounded, and eight ambulances damaged.   On the
5th it was ascertained that the enemy had fallen
back, but it could not be determined whether he was
retreating, or was seeking a more advantageous position.   The Sixth Corps pursued him for some distance, and it was discovered on the 6th that he was
in retreat.   On that day and the next the Army
moved toward the Potomac.   As I was obliged to
leave with the Commanding General, I placed the
wounded under the general charge of Surgeon Henry
Janes, U. S. Volunteers.   Assistant-Surgeon Brinton
was directed to act as Medical Purveyor, and four
wagons and six ambulances from each corps were
ordered to be retained for carrying the supplies to
the hospitals, and the wounded who were to be sent
away, from the hospitals to the railroad depot.   Six
hundred and fifty Medical officers had been busily
employed from the opening of the battle until the
night of the 6th.   Most of the operations had been
performed, and the remaining duties were to dress

the wounds, and perform such operations as, from time to time, were required. One-third of the operating staff, with other Medical officers, numbering over one hundred, were ordered to remain. On July 7th I requested Surgeon-General Hammond to send twenty Surgeons, to report to Dr. Janes. Numbers of Medical men came to that field, after the Army left; some worked devotedly; but the majority "were of little use." It cannot be too strongly impressed upon the Government authorities, that an army must rely upon its own Medical officers for the care of the sick and wounded. Three Surgeons to a regiment, with a proper allowance for administrative duty, should always accompany an army in the field. There will, of course, be frequent occasions when they will have little to do, but on the field of battle that number will not be too great properly to attend the wounded. Many Surgeons in civil life are anxious to operate, and thus assist the wounded, but this is a very small portion of a Surgeon's duties; the latter can only be learned by experience with armies. There should be no sliding scale, where the number of Medical officers varies with the number of men; such a system is a source of perpetual trouble and vexation, and is false economy. The wounded in these three days amounted to fourteen thousand one hundred and ninety-three, and those of the enemy, who fell into our hands, to six thousand eight hundred and two, making twenty thousand nine hundred and ninety-five to be provided for by the Medical Department.

The Army left Gettysburg with the expectation of engaging, within a few days, in another battle, as severe as that which it had just fought, and it was necessary to be prepared for this emergency. A number of Surgeons-in-Chief of Division had replenished their supplies, from those brought to Gettysburg by Dr. Brinton; on July 5th, before the Army left that place, I ordered supplies from Washington to Frederick, Maryland; and on the 6th ordered an additional amount from Philadelphia to the same city, all of which reached their destination in due season. Tents were procured, and all needful arrangements made for another battle. The Army confronted the enemy, near Williamsport, Maryland, until the latter recrossed the Potomac, about the middle of July, when we moved to the vicinity of Harper's Ferry, passing the same stream where we had crossed it a few months before, and marching to Manassas Gap, where a part of the Third Corps had a brisk rencontre with a portion of the enemy's forces guarding this pass. This engagement was known as the battle of Wapping Heights; the wounded were not numerous, and were admirably attended by Assistant-Surgeon

Calhoun, U. S. A., Acting Medical Director of the Corps. It was owing to his care, and that of Captain Webster, of the Ambulance Corps, that they suffered so little while being transported over the road through this gap, which was rougher than any I had ever seen east of the Rocky Mountains. I was surprised to find such a road among civilized people.

The Army encamped for the remainder of the summer near the Rappahannock. Neither army was disposed to assume the offensive during the very warm weather, but remained at rest, giving the troops time to recover from the great exertions they had undergone, and recruit their energies, so largely drawn upon during the late campaign. Assistant-Surgeon McMillin, U. S. A., was, at his own request, relieved from duty as Medical Purveyor. The fidelity and energy with which this young officer performed his duties met my warmest approbation. Wishing to remedy some defects in the Ambulance system I had established in 1862, I revised the order, which, meeting the approval of the Commanding General, was published to the Army. The following is a copy:

11

"AMBULANCE CORPS AND AMBULANCE TRAINS.

"HEADQUARTERS, ARMY OF THE POTOMAC,
August 24, 1863.

" GENERAL ORDERS,
No. 85.

"The following revised regulations for the organization of the Ambulance Corps, and the management of the Ambulance Trains, are published for the government of all concerned, and will be strictly observed:

"1. The Army Corps is the unit of organization for the Ambulance Corps, and the latter will be organized upon the basis of one captain as the commandant of the corps, one first lieutenant for each division, one second lieutenant for each brigade, one sergeant for each regiment.

"2. The privates of this corps will consist of two men and one driver to each ambulance, and one driver to each medicine wagon.

"3. The two-horse ambulances only will be used, and the allowance, until further orders, to each corps, will be upon the basis of three to each regiment of infantry, two to each regiment of cavalry, one to each battery of artillery, to which it will be permanently attached, and two to the headquarters of each army corps, and two army wagons to each division. Each ambulance will be provided with two stretchers.

"4. The captain is the commander of all the ambulances, medicine and other wagons in the corps, under the immediate direction of the Medical Director of the army corps to which the Ambulance Corps belongs. He will pay special attention to the condition of the ambulances, wagons, horses, harness, etc., and see that they are at all times in readiness for service; that the officers and men are properly instructed in their duties, and that these duties are performed, and that the regulations for the corps are strictly adhered to by those under his command. He will institute a drill in his corps, instructing his men in the most easy and expeditious method of putting men in and taking them out of the ambulances, lifting them from the ground, and placing and carrying them on stretchers, in the latter case observing that the front man steps off with the left foot and the rear man with the right, etc.; that in all cases his men treat the sick and wounded with gentleness and care; that the ambulances and wagons are at all times provided with attendants, drivers, horses, etc.; that the vessels for carrying water are constantly kept clean, and filled with fresh water; that the ambulances are not used for any other purpose

than that for which they are designed and ordered.
Previous to a march he will receive from the Medical
Director of the Army Corps his orders for the distribution of the ambulances for gathering up the sick
and wounded; previous to and in time of action, he
will receive orders from the same officer where to
send his ambulances, and to what point the wounded
are to be carried. He will give his personal attention to the removal of the sick and wounded from the
field in time of action, going from place to place to
ascertain what may be wanted; to see that his
subordinates (for whose conduct he will be responsible) attend faithfully to their duties in taking care of
the wounded, and removing them as quickly as may
be found consistent with their safety to the field hospital, and see that the ambulances reach their destination. After every battle he will make a report, in
detail, of the operations of his corps to the Medical
Director of the Army Corps to which he belongs,
who will transmit a copy, with such remarks as he
may deem proper, to the Medical Director of this
Army. He will give his personal attention to the
removal of sick when they are required to be sent to
general hospitals, or to such other points as may be
ordered. He will make a personal inspection, at least
once a month, of every thing pertaining to the Ambulance Corps, a report·of which will be made to the

Medical Director of the Corps, who will transmit a copy to the Medical Director of this Army. This inspection will be minute and made with care, and will not supersede the constant supervision which he must at all times exercise over his corps. He will also make a weekly report, according to the prescribed form, to the same officer, who will forward a copy to the Medical Director of this Army.

" 5. The first lieutenant assigned to the Ambulance Corps for a division will have complete control, under the captain of his corps, and the Medical Director of the Army Corps, of all the ambulances, medicine, and other wagons, horses, etc., and men in that portion of the Ambulance Corps. He will be the Acting Assistant Quartermaster for that portion of the corps, and will receipt for and be responsible for all the property belonging to it, and be held responsible for any deficiency in any thing appertaining thereto. He will have a travelling cavalry forge, a blacksmith, and a saddler, who will be under his orders, to enable him to keep his train in order. His supplies will be drawn from the depot quartermaster, upon requisitions approved by the captain of his corps, and the commander of the army corps to which he is attached. He will exercise a constant supervision over his train in every particular, and keep it at all times ready for service. Especially before a battle will he be careful that every thing be in order. The responsible duties devolving upon him in time of action render it necessary that he be active and vigilant, and spare no labor in their execution. He will make reports to the captain of the corps, upon the forms prescribed, every Saturday morning.

"6. The second lieutenant will have command of the portion of the Ambulance Corps for a brigade, and will be under the immediate orders of the commander of the ambulances for a division, and the injunctions in regard to care and attention, and supervision prescribed for the commander of the division, he will exercise in that portion under his command.

"7. The sergeant will conduct the drills, inspections, etc., under the orders and supervision of the commander of the ambulances for a brigade, be particular in enforcing all orders he may receive from his superior officer, and that the men are attentive to their duties. The officers and non-commissioned officers will be mounted. The non-commissioned officers will be armed with revolvers.

"8. Two Medical officers and two hospital stewards will be detailed daily, by roster, by the Surgeon-in-Chief of Division, to accompany the ambulances for the division when on the march, whose duties will be to attend to the sick and wounded with the ambulances, and see that they are properly cared for. No man will be permitted, by any line officer, to fall to the rear to ride in the ambulances, unless he has written permission, from the senior Medical officer of his regiment, to do so. These passes will be carefully preserved, and at the close of the march be transmitted, by the senior Medical officer with the train, with such remarks as he may deem proper, to the Surgeon-in-Chief of his division. A man who is sick or wounded, who requires to be carried in an ambulance, will not be rejected, should he not have the permission required; the Surgeon of the regiment who has neglected to give it, will be reported at the close of the march, by the senior Surgeon with the train, to the Surgeon-in-Chief of his division. When on the march, one-half of the privates of the Ambulance Corps will accompany, on foot, the ambulances to which they belong, to render such assistance as may be required. The remainder will march in the rear of their respective commands, to conduct, under the order of the Medical officer, such men as may be unable to proceed to the ambulances, or who may be incapable of taking proper care of themselves until the ambulances come up. When the case is of so serious a nature as to require it, the Surgeon of the regiment, or his assistant, will remain and deliver the man to one of the Medical officers with the ambu-

lances. At all other times the privates will be with
their respective trains. The medicine wagons will,
on the march, be in their proper places, in the rear
of the ambulances for each brigade. Upon ordinary
marches, the ambulances and wagons belonging to
the train will follow immediately in the rear of the
division to which it is attached. Officers connected
with the corps must be with the train when on the
march, observing that no one rides in any of the ambulances except by the authority of the Medical
officers. Every necessary facility for taking care of
the sick and wounded upon the march will be
afforded the Medical officers by the officers of the
Ambulance Corps.

" 9. When in camp, the ambulances will be parked
by divisions. The regular roll-calls, reveillé, retreat,
and tattoo, will be held, at which at least one commissioned officer will be present and receive the reports. Stable duty will be at hours fixed by the captain of the corps, and at this time, while the drivers
are in attendance upon their animals, the privates
will be employed in keeping the ambulances to which
they belong in order ; keeping the vessels for carrying
water filled with fresh water, and in general police
duties. Should it become necessary for a regimental
Medical officer to use one or more ambulances for
transporting sick and wounded, he will make a

requisition upon the commander of the ambulances for a division, who will comply with the requisition. In all cases when ambulances are used, the officers, non-commissioned officers, and men belonging to them will accompany them; should one ambulance only be required, a non-commissioned officer, as well as the men belonging to it, will accompany it. The officers of the Ambulance Corps will see that ambulances are not used for any other purposes than that for which they are designed, viz., the transportation of sick and wounded, and, in urgent cases only, for medical supplies. All officers are expressly forbidden to use them, or require them to be used, for any other purpose. When ambulances are required for the transportation of sick or wounded at Division or Brigade headquarters, they will be obtained, as they are needed for this purpose, from the division train; but no ambulances belonging to this corps will be retained at such Headquarters.

" 10. Good, serviceable horses will be used for the ambulances and medicine wagons, and will not be taken for any other purpose except by orders from these headquarters.

" 11. This corps will be designated for sergeants, by a green band, one and a quarter inches broad, around the cap, and chevrons of the same material, with the point toward the shoulder, on each arm above the

elbow. For privates, by a band, the same as for sergeants, around the cap, and a half chevron of the same
material on each arm above the elbow.

"12. No person except the proper Medical officers,
or the officers, non-commissioned officers, and privates
of this corps, will be permitted to take or accompany
sick or wounded to the rear, either on the march or
upon the field of battle.

"13. No officer or man will be selected for this
service except those who are active and efficient,
and they will be detailed by corps commanders
only.

"14. Corps commanders will see that the foregoing regulations are carried into effect.

"By command of Major-General MEADE.

"S. WILLIAMS,
Assistant-Adjutant-General.

It will be perceived that the following Act of
Congress is simply a modification of the preceding
order:

"*An Act to establish a uniform system of Ambulances in the Armies of the United States.*

"*Be it enacted by the Senate and House of Rep-
resentatives of the United States of America in Congress assembled,* That the Medical Director, or Chief

Medical officer of each army corps shall, under the control of the Medical Director of the army to which such army corps belongs, have the direction and supervision of all ambulances, medicine, and other wagons, horses, mules, harness, and other fixtures appertaining thereto, and of all officers and men who may be detailed or employed to assist him in the management thereof, in the army corps in which he may be serving.

"SEC. 2. *And be it further enacted*, That the commanding officer of each army corps shall detail officers and enlisted men for service in the Ambulance Corps of such army corps, upon the following basis, viz., one captain, who shall be commandant of said Ambulance Corps; one first lieutenant for each division in such army corps; one second lieutenant for each brigade in such army corps; one sergeant for each regiment in such army corps; three privates for each ambulance, and one private for each wagon; and the officers and non-commissioned officers of the Ambulance Corps shall be mounted: provided, that the officers, non-commissioned officers, and privates so detailed for each army corps shall be examined by a board of Medical officers of such army corps as to their fitness for such duty; and that such as are found to be not qualified shall be rejected, and others detailed in their stead.

"SEC. 3. *And be it further enacted*, That there shall be allowed and furnished to each army corps two-horse ambulances, upon the following basis, to wit: three to each regiment of infantry of five hundred men or more; two to each regiment of infantry of more than two hundred and not less than five hundred men or more; and one to each regiment of infantry of less than two hundred men; two to each regiment of cavalry of five hundred men or more, and one to each regiment of cavalry of less than five hundred men; one to each battery of artillery, to which battery of artillery it shall be permanently attached; to the headquarters of each Army Corps two such ambulances; and to each division train of ambulances two army wagons; and ambulances shall be allowed and furnished to divisions, brigades, and commands not attached to any army corps upon the same basis; and each ambulance shall be provided with such number of stretchers and other appliances as shall be prescribed by the Surgeon-General: Provided, that the ambulances and wagons herein mentioned shall be furnished, so far as practicable, from the ambulances and wagons now in the service.

"SEC. 4. *And be it further enacted*, That horse and mule litters may be adopted or authorized by the Secretary of War in lieu of ambulances, when judged necessary, under such rules and regulations as may be prescribed by the Medical Director of each Army Corps.

"Sec. 5. *And be it further enacted,* That the captain shall be the commander of all the ambulances, medicine, and other wagons in the Corps, under the immediate direction of the Medical Director or Chief Medical officer of the Army Corps to which the Ambulance Corps belongs. He shall pay special attention to the condition of the ambulances, wagons, horses, mules, harness, and other fixtures appertaining thereto, and see that they are at all times in readiness for service ; that the officers and men of the Ambulance Corps are properly instructed in their duties, and that their duties are performed, and that the regulations which may be prescribed by the Secretary of War or the Surgeon-General for the government of the Ambulance Corps are strictly observed by those under his command. It shall be his duty to institute a drill in his Corps, instructing his men in the most easy and expeditious manner of moving the sick and wounded, and to require in all cases that the sick and wounded shall be treated with gentleness and care, and that the ambulances and wagons are at all times provided with attendants, drivers, horses, mules, and whatever may be necessary for their efficiency ; and it shall be his duty also to see that the ambulances are not used for any other purpose than that for which

they are designed and ordered. It shall be the duty
of the Medical Director or Chief Medical officer of
the Army Corps, previous to a march, and previous to
and in time of action, or whenever it may be necessary to use the ambulances, to issue the proper orders
to the captain for the distribution and management
of the same, for collecting the sick and wounded, and
conveying them to their destination. And it shall
be the duty of the captain faithfully and diligently
to execute such orders. And the officers of the Ambulance Corps, including the Medical Director, shall
make such reports, from time to time, as may be required by the Secretary of War, the Surgeon-General,
the Medical Director of the Army, or the commanding officer of the Corps in which they may be serving;
and all reports to higher authority than the commanding officer of the Army Corps shall be transmitted
through the Medical Director of the Army to which
Army Corps belongs.

"SEC. 6. *And be it further enacted*, That the first
lieutenant assigned to the Ambulance Corps for a
division shall have complete control, under the captain of his corps and the Medical Director of the
Army Corps, of all the ambulances, medicine and
other wagons, horses, mules, and men in that portion
of the Ambulance Corps. He shall be the acting
assistant quartermaster for that portion of the Ambu-

lance Corps, and will receipt for and be responsible for all the property belonging to it, and be held responsible for any deficiency in any thing appertaining thereto. He shall have a travelling cavalry forge, a blacksmith, and a saddler, who shall be under his orders, to enable him to keep his train in order. He shall have authority to draw supplies from the depot quartermaster, upon requisitions approved by the captain of his Corps, the Medical Director, and the commander of the army corps to which he is attached. It shall be his duty to exercise a constant supervision over his train in every particular, and keep it at all times ready for service.

"SEC. 7. *And be it further enacted*, That the second lieutenant shall have command of the portion of the Ambulance Corps for a brigade; and shall be under the immediate orders of the first lieutenant; and he shall exercise a careful supervision over the sergeants and privates assigned to the portion of the Ambulance Corps for his brigade; and it shall be the duty of the sergeants to conduct the drills and inspections of the ambulances, under his orders, of their respective regiments.

"SEC. 8. *And be it further enacted*, That the ambulances in the armies of the United States shall be used only for the transportation of the sick and wounded, and, in urgent cases only, for medical supplies, and all persons shall be prohibited from using them or requiring them to be used for any other purpose. It shall be the duty of the officers of the Ambulance Corps to report to the commander of the army corps any violation of the provisions of this section, or any attempt to violate the same. Any officer who shall use an ambulance, or require it to be used, for any other purpose than as provided in this section, shall, for the first offence, be publicly reprimanded by the commander of the army corps in which he may be serving; and, for the second offence, shall be dismissed from the service.

"SEC. 9. *And be it further enacted,* That no person, except the proper Medical officers, or the officers, non-commissioned officers, and privates of the Ambulance Corps, or such persons as may be specially assigned by competent military authority to duty with the Ambulance Corps, for the occasion, shall be permitted to take or accompany sick or wounded men to the rear, either on the march or upon the field of battle.

"SEC. 10. *And be it further enacted,* That the officers, non-commissioned officers, and privates of the Ambulance Corps shall be designated by such uniform or in such manner as the Secretary of War shall deem proper: provided, that officers and men may be relieved from service in said corps, and others detailed to the same, subject to the examination provided in the second section of this act, in the discretion of the commanders of the armies in which they may be serving.

"SEC. 11. *And be it further enacted,* That it shall be the duty of the commander of the army corps to transmit to the Adjutant-General the names and rank of all officers and enlisted men, detailed for service in the Ambulance Corps of such army corps, stating the organization from which they may have been so detailed; and if such officers and men belong to volunteer organizations, the Adujant-General shall thereupon notify the Governors of the several States in which such organizations were raised, of their detail for such service; and it shall be the duty of the commander of the army corps to report to the Adjutant-General, from time to time, the conduct and behavior of the officers and enlisted men of the Ambulance Corps; and the Adjutant-General shall forward copies of such reports, so far as they relate to the officers and enlisted men of volunteer organizations, to the Governors of the States in which such organizations were raised.

"SEC. 12. *And be it further enacted,* That nothing in this act shall be construed to diminish or impair the rightful authority of the commanders of armies, army corps, or separate detachments, over the Medi-

cal and other officers, and the non-commissioned officers and privates of their respective commands.

"*Approved, March* 11, 1864."

In this law the number of ambulances and men is
not regulated by the number of regiments, but by
the number of men in a regiment, which is subject to
continual variation. The Medical Director cannot
know what transportation he has for the wounded
under such regulation. The number of ambulances
and attendants should be governed by the number
of regiments, and three to each one will not be too
many. The experience of the wounded on the south
side of the Rapidan, during the spring of 1864, con-
firmed the justice of my views. In addition to the
revision of the ambulance system, I arranged with
Brigadier-General Ingalls, Chief Quartermaster, that
all the army wagons mentioned in the order should
be under the exclusive control of the ambulance
officers, whom I also required to be responsible for
the tents, axes, etc., etc., used by the Medical Department. By these means the Medical officers were
relieved from all care of this kind of property, and it
was at the same time removed from the control of
brigade and regimental quartermasters. This was a
very important matter, as it rendered the department,

in a great measure, independent in its transportation.

I purchased flags, having the distinctive mark of each corps in red, white, and blue, according to division. These were carried at the head of each division train of ambulances on the march, and were raised over the division hospitals when in camp, or on the battle-field. Small flags were provided for each Medical Director. I established a system of passes to the ambulance trains, and for passage to general hospitals; a copy of each permit will be found in the Appendix.

On the 3d of September I carefully revised the supply table, and issued a new one, which will be found in the Appendix. About this time I made an ineffectual attempt to have the Medical transportation restored to the allowance of the autumn of 1862. I am still of opinion that the allowance was not more than sufficient; and it is absolutely necessary to the efficiency of any department that its organization, when once properly established, should be permanent. How can the Medical Department of an army discharge its responsible duties when it has not sufficient transportation for its supplies? The long marches through heat and rain, and living on marching rations, had caused symptoms of scurvy, shortly after we encamped for the summer, but they speedily disappeared

after the use of fresh vegetables and bread, and the
lemons which the Medical Purveyor purchased by
my directions. The heat, bad water, and the miasma
of the low grounds along the Rappahannock, increased
to some extent the number of cases of fevers, but the
majority recovered, and in October these diseases
almost entirely ceased.

In the month of September there was much skir-
mishing by the cavalry (chiefly under Brigadier-General Buford), on the south side of the Rappahannock,
and in the direction of Culpepper Court House. And
about the middle of the month, the whole Army
moved to the vicinity of that town, the enemy retreating to the right bank of the Rapidan. Sharing
in the very general impression that a severe engagement would take place upon our arrival in that section of the country, I ordered the Medical Purveyor,
with his abundant supplies, to proceed to Culpepper,
placed the department in readiness for the anticipated
conflict, and so arranged it as to take care of the
wounded in the event of a battle, or move them
speedily to the rear, should military necessity require
such a course. No engagement took place, but on
the 9th of October the enemy was discovered moving
on our right, which compelled us to fall back to the
heights of Centreville. In this movement the Second
Corps had a sharp encounter, near Catlett's Station,

with the enemy, in which the latter was repulsed. Upon the arrival of the Army at Centreville, the enemy retired, destroying the railroad as far as the Rappahannock, upon which stream he remained until early in November, when he was driven from it, and again took up his position on the south side of the Rapidan.

At this time portions of our troops had frequent encounters with small bodies of the enemy, in which there were few wounded. Nothing of particular interest occurred in the Medical Department, now equal to any emergency.

On the 24th of November the Army, without resistance, crossed the Rapidan, to drive the enemy from the position he held on that "dark and bloody ground" the Wilderness. Shortly after crossing the river the Third Corps, under Major-General French, was vigorously but unsuccessfully attacked by a large body of the enemy. Here we had eight hundred wounded, who, in spite of the inclement weather, were well taken care of by Surgeon A. Chapel, U. S. Volunteers, the Medical Director of that Corps.

The enemy was found posted on a range of hills, on the west of Mine Run, on the eastern side of which our Army was drawn up in line of battle. The position of the enemy was strong by nature, and made still stronger by art, and had we attacked him, we should in all probability have been unsuccessful.

Under these circumstances it required high moral courage in a Commanding General to order a retreat; in Major-General Meade that courage was fortunately found, and the Army retired, during the night of December 1st, to its former camp on the north side of the Rapidan. The weather was now very cold and wet, and the troops being without shelter suffered severely, several men on the line of skirmishers confronting the enemy having been frozen to death. When it was known where the corps would be posted in the line of battle, the division hospitals, designated by their flags, were made ready for the reception of the wounded; and although the position of some of the corps was frequently changed, the hospitals (also changed) were well fitted up with straw, blankets, and surgical appliances; most of them had fire-places, built of sticks and mud, so that the wounded would have been made quite comfortable.

Upon our return to camp, my attention was once more given to the preservation of the health of the troops, who, I saw, would be compelled to go into winter quarters. My views on this matter have been so fully given, that I refrain from further allusion to the subject.

The amount of brandy and whiskey used in the Medical Department appeared to me excessive; it led to hasty and therefore incomplete examination of cases of disease. It is easy, in a case with a weak pulse, to prescribe stimulants, and this practice accords with the ideas of unprofessional persons, and the cause of the disease is apt to overlooked. With the view of confining the expenditure of these articles to cases in which they were really required, I directed reports of such issues to be sent me every week, the form for which can be seen in the Appendix. If any doubt arose as to the proper use of them in any regiment, that command was at once inspected. The issues of medical and surgical supplies to the whole army were carefully examined in the Medical Director's office every month, by which means I was always informed of the state of supplies throughout the department.

In the latter part of December I purchased a large amount of jellies, fruits, and poultry for the use of the sick, most of whom were kept with their commands, and the hospitals were supplied daily with fresh oysters.

At the close of 1863 the Army was in better health than it had been since the Peninsular Campaign; in July, 1862, it had a large percentage of sick; the beginning of 1864 found it with a very

small one—if my memory be correct, about three per cent.

During the summer and autumn the Cavalry had frequent engagements with the enemy. The wounded were carefully attended by Surgeon G. L. Pancoast, U. S. Volunteers, who very successfully administered the Medical Department of this Corps. The cavalry service required Medical officers freely to expose themselves, and Assistant-Surgeons McGill, Notson, and Forwood, of the Regular Army, and Surgeon Walborn of the Seventeenth Pennsylvania Cavalry, were wounded in the storms of shot and shell which they fearlessly encountered in their duties to the wounded. It gives me very great pleasure to recall the services of Hospital Steward Robert Koldeway, U. S. A., who was constantly with me. The intelligence, alacrity, and zeal shown at all times by this non-commissioned officer, in the discharge of the laborious duties required of him in the Medical Director's office, were worthy of all commendation.

It was evident that no military movements could be made by either army, the season of the year would effectually prevent them. The Medical Department had been completely organized in all its branches, the method of supplying had been changed, and so arranged that Medical officers could be at all times well provided; the field hospitals had been instituted, to the great advantage of the wounded; an ambulance system had been established, which operated well. Little more remained to be done, beyond the ordinary routine of duties.

The Massachusetts troops in the Army of the Potomac owe much to Surgeon-General Dale, of that State, for the great care he displayed in the selection of their Medical officers. His requirements were, ability and attention to duty; and it would have been well had such qualifications only been considered everywhere, in the appointment of officers so important to the well-being of an army.

In all my duties I received most valuable assistance from Assistant-Medical Director Clements; his unwearied industry, and unfailing devotion to duty, and his ability, called forth my admiration, while his kindness of heart and refinement of feeling awakened a friendship that can never be broken.

Early in January, 1864, I was relieved, at my own request, from the position of Medical Director, and my connection with the Army of the Potomac ceased. For eighteen months of arduous and eventful service, I had shared the varying fortunes of that gallant Army, and formed many warm friendships with its best and bravest, some of whom were not fated to accompany their comrades, on many a bloody field, to the final triumph that purchased our peace, and restored our Union.

But whether the grass grows over them, or they are wanderers, far from the scene of their perils and victories, those who labored together with but one heart, in their country's hour of agony, will live among the many memories that cluster around the dear old Army of the Potomac.

APPENDIX.

ARMY OF THE POTOMAC.

Report of the Sick and Wounded for the Week ending Saturday the ———— day of ———————— 186 .

COMMAND.	Mean aggregate strength of the Command present during the week.	Unfit for duty at last Weekly Report.	Taken sick during the week.	Wounded during the week.	Total unfit for duty during the week.	Returned to duty during the week.	Discharged the service during the week.	Sent to General Hospital during the week.	Sent on furlough on account of sickness during the week.	Died during the week.	Remaining unfit for duty at the date of this Report.
TOTAL.											

REMARKS.

(Signature) ....

REPORT of the Medical Inspector of the.......Corps, Army

DATE OF INSPECTION.	DIVISION.	BRIGADE.	REGIMENT.			MEDICAL OFFICERS.				HOSPITAL STEWARDS.		AVERAGE NUMBER ON SICK REPORT DAILY FOR THE MONTH PRECEDING DATE OF INSPECTION.			Daily Ratio of Sick per 1,000 of average aggregate strength present during the month.	PREVAILING DISEASES.
						PRESENT		ABSENT								
			Designation.	Date of Entry into Service.	Average aggregate strength present during the month preceding date of Inspection.	For Duty.	Sick.	On Leave.	Detached.	Present.	Absent.	In Hospital.	In Quarters.	Total.		

NOTE: The Report will exhibit the condition of *each Regiment.* The condition will invariably be
    In the column "Medical and Hospital Supplies," the letters "F" and "D" will express
    In the column "Records," their completeness or incompleteness will be expressed by the

of the **Potomac**, for the month ending.......................1863.

CONDITION OF CAMP AND QUARTERS.									CONDITION OF HOSPITAL.														REMARKS.
QUARTERS.		COOKING.		POLICE.																				
Kind.	Condition.	By Squads.	By Companies.	Personal.	Camp.	Water.	Drainage.	Sinks.	Site.	Water.	Drainage.	Sinks.	Police.	No. of Tents.	No. of Huts or Houses.	Ventilation.	How Warmed.	Cooking.	Cleanliness of Patients.	No. of Attendants.	Medical and Hospital Supplies.	Records.	

pressed as "Good," "Fair," and "Bad," by the letters "G," "F," and "B."
.ether the supply is full or deficient.
tors "C" or "I," in addition to the letter expressing the *manner* in which they are kept.

....
Medical Inspector............*Corps.*

LIST OF WOUNDED in the Hospital of the_____
of_____on the

No.	NAMES.		RANK.	CO.	REGIMENT.	CORPS.
	SURNAME.	CHRISTIAN NAME.				

NOTE.—This List will be made with the strictest accuracy, and will be transmitted by the Medical Directors of Grand Divisions to the Medical Director of the Army, *within seven days* after an engagement. The names of all men treated in the Hospital will be entered upon this List. When men are transferred to or from other Division Hospitals, the fact of the transfer and the date will be noted in the " Remarks."

Division_____Corps, Army of the Potomac, at the Battle
_____day of_____, 186 .

INJURY.		TREATMENT.	RESULT, AND DATE OF.	REMARKS.
Seat of.	Nature of.			

....

Surgeon-in-Chief, ... Division, ... Corps.

*REPORT of aggregate strength for duty, and names of Medical Officers present for duty,
and the killed, wounded, and missing in the battle of............on the............
day of............1863, according to Regimental Reports, of the..............
Division,............Corps.*

REGIMENTS.	Aggregate strength present for duty.	Names of Surgeons present for Duty.	Names of Assistant Surgeons present for Duty.	Number killed according to Regimental Report.	Number wounded according to Regimental Report.	Number missing according Regimental Report.
TOTAL............						

....

Surgeon-in-Chief,........Division,........Corps.

TABULAR STATEMENT *of Wounded in the Hospital of the....Division....Corps, Army of the Potomac, at the Battle of........, on the....day of......., 186 .*

REGION OF BODY WOUNDED.		MISSILE OR WEAPON.							OPERATIONS.			ANÆS-THETICS.		REMARKS.
		Cannon Ball.	Shell.	Bullet.	Sword.	Bayonet.	Other.	TOTAL.	Amputations.	Exsections.	Other.	Given in.	Deaths from	
	Head													
	Face													
	Neck													
	Chest..............													
	Abdomen..........													
	Back and Spine.....													
	Hips and Genitals..													
	Shoulder...........													
ARM. {	Flesh Wound.......													
	Fracture...........													
	Elbow joint........													
FOREARM. {	Flesh wound.......													
	Fracture...........													
	Wrist....													
	Hand..............													
THIGH. {	Hip joint...........													
	Flesh Wound													
	Fracture, upper 3d..													
	" mdle 3d..													
	" lower 3d..													
	Knee joint.........													
LEG. {	Flesh Wound.......													
	Fracture...........													
	Ankle joint													
	Foot...............													
INJURIES OF ARTER-IES AND NERVES. {														

.... *Surgeon-in Chief,*
............*Division........Corps.*

NOTE.—This Statement will be transmitted by the Medical Directors of Corps to the Medical Director of the Army *within three days* after an engagement. No excuse will be received for failure in its transmittal within the time here directed,

Sent to General Hospital.

No. _____

Date, _____186

Name, _____

Rank, _____ Comp. _____ Regt.

Brig. _____ Div. _____ Corps.

Disease, _____

No. _____

Date, _____186

Name, _____

Rank, _____ Comp. _____ Regt.

Brig. _____ Div. _____ Corps.

Disease, _____

FOR GENERAL HOSPITAL.

No. _____   Date, _____186

Authority is given to send _____ of

_____ Comp. _____ Regt. _____ Brig. _____ Divis. _____ Corps,

the bearer of this pass, to General Hospital.

Not Transferable.

_____ **Surgeon.**

Surg. in Chief _____ Div. _____ Corps.

No. _____

Date, _____186

_____ Brigade, _____ Division, _____ Corps,

Pass _____ of Comp. _____ Regt. _____

for admission to the Ambulance Train,

_____

Surgeon _____ Regt.

NOW COMPLETE.

THE NEW AMERICAN CYCLOPÆDIA,

A POPULAR DICTIONARY OF GENERAL KNOWLEDGE.

EDITED BY

GEORGE RIPLEY AND C. A. DANA,

ASSISTED BY A NUMEROUS BUT SELECT CORPS OF WRITERS.

The design of THE NEW AMERICAN CYCLOPÆDIA is to furnish the great body of intelligent readers in this country with a popular Dictionary of General Knowledge.

THE NEW AMERICAN CYCLOPÆDIA is not founded on any European model; in its plan and elaboration it is strictly original, and strictly American. Many of the writers employed on the work have enriched it with their personal researches, observations, and discoveries; and every article has been written, or re-written, expressly for its pages.

It is intended that the work shall bear such a character of practical utility as to make it indispensable to every American library.

Throughout its successive volumes, THE NEW AMERICAN CYCLOPÆDIA will present a fund of accurate and copious information on SCIENCE, ART, AGRICULTURE, COMMERCE, MANUFACTURES, LAW, MEDICINE, LITERATURE, PHILOSOPHY, MATHEMATICS, ASTRONOMY, HISTORY, BIOGRAPHY, GEOGRAPHY, RELIGION, POLITICS, TRAVELS, CHEMISTRY, MECHANICS, INVENTIONS, and TRADES.

Abstaining from all doctrinal discussions, from all sectional and sectarian arguments, it will maintain the position of absolute impartiality on the great controverted questions which have divided opinions in every age.

PRICE.

This work is published exclusively by subscription, in sixteen large octavo volumes, each containing 750 two-column pages.

Price per volume, cloth, $5.00; library style, leather, $6.00; half morocco, $6.50; half russia, extra, $7.50.

From the London Daily News.

It is beyond all comparison the best,—indeed, we should feel quite justified in saying it is the only book of reference upon the Western Continent that has ever appeared. No statesman or politician can afford to do without it, and it will be a treasure to every student of the moral and physical condition of America. Its information is minute, full, and accurate upon every subject connected with the country. Beside the constant attention of the Editors, it employs the pens of a host of the most distinguished transatlantic writers—statesmen, lawyers, divines, soldiers, a vast array of scholarship from the professional chairs of the Universities, with numbers of private literati, and men devoted to special pursu'ts.

A STANDARD BOOK OF REFERENCE.

THE

HOUSEHOLD BOOK OF POETRY.

Collected and Edited by CHARLES A. DANA.

Tenth Edition.   Royal 8vo.   798 pages.   Beautifully printed.

Half mor., gilt top, $6; half calf, extra, $7.50; mor. ant., $10.

"The purpose of this book is to comprise within the bounds of a single volume whatever is truly beautiful and admirable among the minor poems of the English language. * * * Especial care has also been taken to give every poem entire and unmutilated, as well as in the most authentic form which could be procured."—*Extract from Preface.*

"This work is an immense improvement on all its predecessors. The editor, who is one of the most erudite of scholars, and a man of excellent taste, has arranged his selections under ten heads, namely: Poems of Nature, of Childhood, of Friendship, of Love, of Ambition, of Comedy, of Tragedy and Sorrow, of the Imagination, of Sentiment and Reflection, and of Religion. The entire number of poems given is about two thousand, taken from the writings of English and American poets, and including some of the finest versions of poems from ancient and modern languages. The selections appear to be admirably made, nor do we think that it would be possible for any one to improve upon this collection."—*Boston Traveller.*

"Within a similar compass, there is no collection of poetry in the language that equals this in variety, in richness of thought and expression, and of poetic imagery."—*Worcester Palladium.*

"This is a choice collection of the finest poems in the English language, and supplies in some measure the place of an extensive library. Mr. Dana has done a capital service in bringing within the reach of all the richest thoughts that grace our standard poetical literature."—*Chicago Press.*

"A work that has long been required, and, we are convinced from the selections made, and the admirable manner in which they are arranged, will commend itself at once to the public."—*Detroit Advertiser.*

"Never was a book more appropriately named. By the exercise of a sound and skilful judgment, and a thorough familiarity with the poetical productions of all nations, the compiler of this work has succeeded in combining, within the space of a single volume, nearly every poem of established worth and compatible length in the English language."—*Philadelphia Journal.*

"It gives us in an elegant and compact form such a body of verse as can be found in no other volume or series of volumes. It is by far the most complete collection that has ever been made of English lyrical poetry."—*Boston Transcript.*

"Among the similar works which have appeared we do not hesitate to give this the highest place."—*Providence Journal.*

"We are acquainted with no selections which, in point of completeness and good taste, excel the 'Household Book of Poetry.'"—*Northwestern Home Journal.*

"It is almost needless to say that it is a mine of poetic wealth."—*Boston Post.*

D. APPLETON & CO.'S PUBLICATIONS.

SOUTH AMERICAN TRAVEL.

WHAT I SAW

ON THE

West Coast of South and North America,

AND AT THE

HAWAIIAN ISLANDS.

BY

H. WILLIS BAXLEY, M. D.

One volume, 8vo. 632 pages. Illustrated. Price, $.

LITERATURE IN LETTERS;

OR,

MANNERS, ART, CRITICISM, BIOGRAPHY, HISTORY AND MORALS,

ILLUSTRATED IN

THE CORRESPONDENCE OF EMINENT PERSONS.

EDITED BY

JAMES P. HOLCOMBE, LL.D.

1 vol., large 12mo. 520 pages, handsomely printed on tinted paper. Cloth extra, gilt top. Price $3.50.

"Such letters," says Lord Bacon, "as are written from wise men, are, of all the words of man, in my judgment the best; for they are more natural than orations and public speeches, and more advised than conferences or private ones." The sources of pleasure and instruction to be found in the private correspondence of eminent persons have never been fully explained; much less have they been rendered accessible to the bulk of the reading public. Our language abounds in letters which contain the most vivid pictures of manners, and the most faithful and striking delineations of character, which are full of wit, wisdom, fancy, useful knowledge, noble and pious sentiment."— *Extract from Preface.*

"The idea of this work is a happy one, and it has been well carried out by the accomplished editor. To concentrate in one compact volume the cream and marrow of a hundred different letter-writers, whose epistles fill many hundred tomes, involved the necessity of a course of reading so extensive that most people would shrink from undertaking it; Dr. Holcombe, however, has accomplished the task, and here presents us with the golden grain, winnowed from the masses of chaff that he has dared to encounter in his progress."—*New York Times.*

"This volume, which, by the way, is very handsomely issued in all respects—is constructed on a novel plan, with entire success. The work is divided into six books: the first comprising 'letters of gossip, society, and manners;' the second 'pleasantry, sentiment, and fancy;' the third 'nature, art, and travel;' the fourth 'those of public history;' the fifth 'literary biography, anecdote, and criticism;' and the sixth 'moral and devotional reflection.' Thus it will be seen that we have here the most interesting topics of life, treated of not in the cold form of essay, but in special letters written warm from one mind to another. All the great letter-writers in our language are represented whose names are 'household words.' "—*Boston Journal.*

"This is one of the most charming books in the language. Dr. Holcombe has taken the most sprightly, racy, readable letters, abounding in wit, fancy, anecdote, allusions to men, women, and events—just the reading that intelligent, cultivated people most admire. It is issued in beautiful dress, and will easily find its way to the hands of thousands of delighted readers."—*New York Observer.*

"This is an extremely interesting work, and gives an insight into the private thoughts and feelings of some of the greatest authors and prominent men and women of the last century. The sources of pleasure and instruction to be found in the private correspondence of eminent persons, have never been fully explored, much less have they been rendered accessible to the bulk of the reading public. His task has been a laborious one, and eminently successful. We commend the volume as a valuable addition to the list of American publications, and worthy a place in the library of every household."— *St. Louis Press.*

AUTOBIOGRAPHY OF MRS. SIGOURNEY.

LETTERS OF LIFE.

By MRS. L. H. SIGOURNEY.

1 vol., 12mo. 414 pages, with Portrait. Cloth. Price $2.00.

" This handsome volume is an autobiography of the authoress, addressed in the form of letters to her cherished friend, Mrs. Caroline Washburne, at whose suggestion they were commenced, and to whom the work, completed by a sketch of Mrs. Sigourney's last days, is dedicated by her daughter. Of all Mrs. Sigourney's numerous works, it is probably the one destined to endure the longest."—*New York Times.*

" One of the pleasantest of Mrs. Sigourney's works has been reserved to appear posthumously, with the above title, and to delight the many admirers of our Hartford poetess. These letters have nothing of the epistolary form but the name, and constitute an autobiography the most charming we have ever read. Mrs. Sigourney portrays the incidents, feelings, and actions of her life from the earliest recollections, giving the whole the fascination of a story added to the spirit of truthful narration which pervades the book."—*Hartford Courant.*

" One of the purest characters as well as one of the most noteworthy among early American writers was Mrs. Sigourney. In days a good while gone by, her volumes were an almost resistless attraction. This volume, compiled by her daughter, is one of rare interest. Its home pictures are charming, its reminiscences fairly sparkle, while its literary merits are of high order. The ' Letters of Life ' will be read eagerly and with delight by thousands."—*Christian Advocate.*

" This is one of the most attractive books of the kind which has issued from the press this many a day. Written in her charming style, the review of the past fifty years, from her position, is absorbingly interesting. She begins with describing her early years, giving an account of her Teachers, her First Journey, Household Employments, her Love and Marriage, her Literary Labors, associates, and publications."—*Boston Recorder.*

" These ' letters,' written by the gifted and useful pen of Mrs. Sigourney, will be, we are inclined to think, the most enduring of her works. They give most interesting and profitable interior views of domestic life, embracing in their survey a kind of biography of their author, interspersed with choice specimens of her literary and poetical productions, and many amusing reminiscences of her long and industrious life."—*New York Observer.*

THE HISTORY

OF

HENRY THE FIFTH:

KING OF ENGLAND, LORD OF IRELAND, AND HEIR OF FRANCE.

By GEORGE MAKEPEACE TOWLE,

AUTHOR OF "GLIMPSES OF HISTORY."

One large volume, 8vo. Elegantly printed on thick tinted paper, embellished with
a steel portrait of Henry the Fifth, and a fac-simile of his autograph.
Cloth. Price, $5.00.

" This very attractive volume is a most valuable contribution to our historical and
biographical literature, and will be read with great interest. The author fully under-
stands his subject, and the times of which he writes, and has given us a work which,
while it has all the fascination and interest of romance, consists of sober, veritable
facts. But few works of the kind have been published for a long time that deserve a
wider circulation."—*Boston Journal.*

" This History describes a remarkable reign in England. It was at the period when
Western Europe was passing out of feudalism and crystallizing about monarchical institutions. The military glory of England was at its zenith. The Reformation of Wick-
liffe was paving the way for further revolutions in Church forms. Mr. Towle has prepared this History with care and fidelity, and has drawn a character which has had few
imitators among the occupants of the British throne."—*New York Commercial Advertiser.*

" The author of this work has sought to fill a vacant space in history. There is no
reliable history of Henry the Fifth of England extant. This historian has added an
interesting and valuable contribution to the number of those works which have been
written by Americans to illustrate periods in modern history."—*New York Observer.*

" The portion of history which he has chosen to illustrate is one of the most ro-
mantic and interesting in all the long story of English progress. It is replete with ad-
venture, sentiments, heroic character, and deeds, great battles and momentous convul-
sions of States. It is singular how little is known of this magnificent reign; how much
that is new to us there is in the work before us, which ought to be familiar as household words. Certainly Mr. Towle has had rare success in so presenting every subject and
event, that there is a glow on his pages which might lead us to believe we were perus-
ing a contemporary narrative. The succession of events is drawn with a dramatic
force which almost ranks the author with the best historians of the time."—*Boston
Post.*

" The materials for this interesting volume are gathered from the writings of those
who lived in his time and soon after, and who treated of the king in treating of other
subjects. The book is ably written, and profoundly interesting. Its value to the
library cannot be estimated."—*Rochester Union.*

CPSIA information can be obtained
at www.ICGtesting.com
Printed in the USA
BVHW040958210620
582000BV00008B/37